CHRISTMAS MISCELLANY

EVERYTHING YOU ALWAYS WANTED
TO KNOW ABOUT CHRISTMAS

CHRISTMAS MISCELLANY

EVERYTHING YOU ALWAYS WANTED TO KNOW ABOUT CHRISTMAS

JONATHAN GREEN

Skyhorse Publishing

Skyhorse Publishing books may be purchased in bulk at special discounts for sales promotion, corporate gifts, fund-raising, or educational purposes. Special editions can also be created to specifications. For details, contact the Special Sales Department, Skyhorse Publishing, 555 Eighth Avenue, Suite 903, New York, NY 10018 or info@skyhorsepublishing.com.

www.skyhorsepublishing.com

10 9 8 7 6 5 4 3 2

Library of Congress Cataloging-in-Publication Data

Green, Jonathan.
    Christmas miscellany : everything you always wanted to know about Christmas / Jonathan Green.
        p. cm.
    ISBN 978-1-60239-757-6
    1. Christmas--Miscellanea. 2. Questions and answers. I. Title.
    GT4985.G73 2009
    394.2663—dc22

                                2009022234

Printed in China

For Mum, who made Christmases past such a wonderful and memorable time, and for Clare, Jake, and Mattie, who mean that Christmas is still something to look forward to today.

CONTENTS

CHRISTMAS MISCELLANY

EVERYTHING YOU ALWAYS WANTED TO KNOW ABOUT CHRISTMAS

INTRODUCTION

At Christmas play and make good cheer,
For Christmas comes but once a year.

The Christmas that we celebrate today is a creation of the past as much as it is a thing of the present. The customs that we keep are an amalgamation of the practices of other times, cultures, religions, and countries. Such diverse groups as the Romans, the Vikings, the peoples of Medieval Europe, and the Victorians, and such faraway places as Germany, Holland, and the Middle East have all had as big an impact on the creation and evolution of Christmas as have the birth of the baby Jesus, the Bible, and the Holy Land.

Indeed, many of the Christmas customs we keep today have their origins thousands of years before Jesus Christ was even born, when people worshipped the sun as the giver of life. And yet, most of us keep these customs without knowing, or even wondering, why.

Why do we put up Christmas trees, send Christmas cards, stuff ourselves with turkey, and hang up stockings on Christmas Eve? You might answer by saying that it's traditional, or simply because it's Christmas. But how have these traditions come about in the first place?

And then there are the fascinating facts about Christmas that have been forgotten in this modern age. Did you know that the first Christmas lights used to adorn a tree belonged to Thomas Edison, or that Santa Claus's official post office is in Finland?

To give you an example of the sort of thing we hope to enlighten you about during the course of this little delight of a book, and to quote the classic Monty Python's *Life of Brian*, "What is myrrh anyway?"

WHAT IS MYRRH ANYWAY?

Everybody has heard of gold, frankincense, and myrrh in the context of the Christmas story. They were, of course, the gifts brought to the baby Jesus by the three wise men. There probably isn't anyone who doesn't know what gold is (a relatively rare, shiny yellow metal, chemical symbol Au), but what of frankincense and, in particular, myrrh?

Of the two, frankincense is the better known. It is a type of incense made from the aromatic resin of the *Boswellia* tree. It was introduced to Europe by Frankish crusaders (hence its name) and used lavishly in religious rituals. When blocks of the hardened resin are burnt, the frankincense gives off a sweet-smelling smoke.

Myrrh is also a type of incense. *Commiphora myrrha* is a thorny shrub native to Somalia and the eastern reaches of Ethiopia. Today, it can also be found growing in other parts of the world, particularly the Arabian Peninsula, as it has been introduced to these regions over the years. However, at the time of Christ's birth, part of what made myrrh so valuable was the distances that had to be traveled to get ahold of the stuff.

Myrrh, as it would have been given to the infant Jesus, is the dried sap of the shrub, a resinous material, reddish-brown in color. The clearer the resin and the darker it is, the better the quality. The scent of raw myrrh is sharp and pleasant but also slightly bitter. The smoke it produces when burnt is also quite bitter, but with a sweet, tarry odor and notes of vanilla.

Its enduring connection has always been with funerals and cremations, hence its prophetic significance as one of the gifts given to Jesus. Up until the fifteenth century it was used as an embalming ointment.

Did you know . . .?

Each of the three gifts given to the Christ child by the wise men had symbolic significance. Gold was a symbol of kingship and glory, but also of Christ's divinity. Frankincense, as the perfume used in ritual worship, stood for both purity and ascending prayer, and spoke of Christ's godhead and godliness. Myrrh, the fragrant burial ointment, was a symbol of Christ's mortality, foretelling his death on the cross, and ultimately his resurrection.

Both myrrh and frankincense are collected in the same way. Delicate incisions are made into the bark of the tree using a special tool. The milky sap that exudes from these incisions hardens as soon as it comes into contact with the air, forming "tears" that are then collected two weeks later. This process is called "tapping." Once collected, the resin is stored for twelve weeks, giving it time to harden completely. The globules of resin are then sorted and graded, a process usually undertaken by the merchant buying it from the collector.

Gum resins were first collected in this way in Arabia, a region that one ancient chronicler, Diodorus Siculus, described as exuding "a most delicate fragrance; even the sailors passing by Arabia can smell the strong fragrance that gives health and vigor."

Myrrh was highly prized in ancient times and was literally worth more than its weight in gold. In ancient Rome it cost five times as much as frankincense, although the latter was by far the more popular.

Myrrh's connection with Christ doesn't begin and end with the gifts given by the wise men. According to the Gospel of Mark, it was also offered to Jesus mingled with wine as he hung in agony from the cross at his crucifixion, the intention being to numb the pain he was feeling. This practice of using myrrh as an additive to wine was common in the ancient world and has even lasted to this day in certain parts of the globe. Myrrh was also used to anoint Jesus's body after his death.

You probably wouldn't be surprised to learn that something so rare and highly valued in ages past is much more widely available today. However, you might be surprised to discover that it is quite possible that you have some lying around the house yourself. It is found in everything from perfumes and lotions to toothpastes and mouthwashes; its antiseptic properties help treat and prevent gum disease. Nursing mothers have known of its analgesic properties for a long time as well, rubbing it onto babies' gums to relieve the pain they feel when teething.

As well as its connections with Christmas through the story of the Nativity, myrrh also has a link to Santa Claus—or at least the fourth-century bishop Saint Nicholas, who inspired the festive gift-giver. It was said that healing myrrh flowed from the saint's sacred relics. Pilgrims seeking such miraculous healing at his shrine would pray to Saint Nicholas as follows:

> With divine myrrh the divine grace of the Spirit anointed thee, who didst preside as the leader of Myra, and having made the ends of the world fragrant with the myrrh of virtues, thou holiest of men, through the pleasant breathings of thine intercessions always driving away the evil stench of the passions. Therefore, in faith we render thee great praise, and celebrate thine all-holy memory, O Nicholas.

WHY IS CHRISTMAS CELEBRATED ON DECEMBER 25?

Let's clear one thing up before we go any further. Why is Christmas celebrated on December 25? Well, it's because December 25 is the date of Jesus's birth, isn't it? No, it isn't. Contrary to popular belief, December 25 is not Jesus Christ's birthday. Oh, and he wasn't born in AD 0 either.

In AD 525, Pope John I charged the scholar Dionysius Exiguus with the task of producing a feast calendar for the Church. Dionysius also estimated the year of Christ's birth but, due to a number of mistakes in his math, he arrived at a date that was a few years shy of the actual event.

So, let's look at the facts.

First of all, the year of Jesus's birth. He was probably born in 6 BC—that's six years before the birth of Christ, believe it or not! Historians have worked this out from the fact that Jesus was born at the time of a Roman census, when "[a] decree went out from the Emperor Caesar Augustus that all the world should be taxed."

The Romans were meticulous about record-keeping, as well as making sure that their taxes were collected, and we know that they carried out censuses of the Empire in 20 BC, 6 BC, and AD 8. Cross-referencing these with other historical facts, such as the reign of King Herod, it is most likely that 6 BC was the year of Christ's birth. But what of the actual date?

We can't be certain of that, but the best guess that scholars can make is that Jesus was probably born in the spring. The Gospel of Saint Luke relates that when the shepherds were told of Christ's birth, they were "out in the fields, keeping watch over their flock by night." Now, even in the Holy Land, you wouldn't want to be out in the open keeping an eye on your sheep in the middle of winter. This was the sort of thing that would happen in the spring, at lambing time.

It might seem incredible to us now, when December 25 is so linked to celebrating the birth of Christ, but for early Christians Christmas itself was not celebrated in any special way. Little fuss was made of the date, which wasn't even fixed at any particular time of year! For these Christians, the most important time in the Church calendar was Easter, when Christ's conquest of death and subsequent resurrection were celebrated.

In fact, early Christians proposed two entirely different dates for Christ's birth. In the tradition of adapting existing pagan festivals to become Christian ones, some early Christians wanted to celebrate the birth of Jesus on January 6. This date was proposed by some because it was when the Egyptians observed the festival of the virgin-goddess Kore, while others believed it to be the birthday of Osiris, god of the underworld (and the first Egyptian mummy), who had himself risen again from the dead (albeit with the assistance of his sister-wife Isis).

However, another group wanted to make March 25 the special day on which to commemorate Christ's birth, as this, according to the Ancient Roman calendar, was the date of the spring equinox. This event symbolized the rebirth of the earth, and one Roman writer, Hippolytus (c. AD 170–235), even worked it out to be the anniversary of God's creation of the world itself. A document supposedly written by one Theophilus of Antioch (AD 171–83) is one of the earliest recognized references to December 25 being the date of Jesus's birth. In the third century AD, December 25 was already a recognized festival, and one that commemorated a special birth. It was the birthday of Mithras, the Persian god of the sun. The cult of Mithras had been brought back to the heart of the Roman Empire by soldiers who had been serving in Syria. There are many surprising similarities between the life of Christ and that of the mythical Mithras.

Mithras was born in a cave, as was Jesus (according to both the *Protoevangelium of James* and *Justin Martyr* from the second century, as this was the typical location of stables in classical Palestine). Mithras sacrificed a bull, from the blood of which sprang the whole of creation, just as God, Jesus's father, had created the world. At the end of his life, Mithras took part in a feast, just as Jesus took part in the Last Supper, before being taken up into heaven in a fiery chariot, just as Jesus ascended to heaven after his resurrection from the dead.

Nonetheless, it wasn't until the year AD 350 that the then Pope, Julius I, made it official. He decreed that Christ's birth would be celebrated on December 25 because it would make it as easy as possible for those Romans who were still pagans (which was most of them) to make the change to the new rituals. The first official mention of there being a Feast of the Nativity on December 25 is in a document known as the Philocalian Calendar, dating from AD 354, but which makes reference to an older document from AD 336. So we at least know that by 354 the celebration of Christmas had become an annual event.

But what of our name for this festival; where did that come from? The first written reference we have to the word "Christmas" itself being used comes from a Saxon book dating from 1038 that mentions *Cristes Maesse*, meaning "Christ's Mass," from which we get "Christmas."

Christmas itself is predated by two major pagan festivals, the Roman Saturnalia and the Viking Yule. Saturnalia was characterized by its turning of the established order on its head, with servants becoming the masters and vice versa. Its legacy lived on in the medieval Christmas when a Lord of Misrule was appointed to oversee the often noisy and disorderly festive celebrations.

It is thought that these midwinter festivals were transformed into Christmas celebrations after the arrival of Saint Augustine in England, at the end of the sixth century, and the subsequent widespread adoption of Christianity by the British. Certainly Christmas Day AD 598 was marked by a spectacular event, when more than 10,000 Englishmen were baptized as Christians.

Some pagan customs were adopted by Christianity in part to help people accept the new religion and convert to it willingly, it being easier and less antagonistic to apply Christian meanings and symbolism to the old rituals than to try simply to stamp them out.

Did you know . . ?

The Holy Roman Empire, an attempt to resurrect the Empire in the West, was established in AD 800 when Pope Leo III crowned Frankish King Charlemagne as Roman Emperor on Christmas Day, though the Empire and the imperial office did not become formalized for some decades.

So, apart from the Persian sun god Mithras, who else was born on Christmas Day? Well, according to the law of averages, plenty of people have been denied the pleasure of receiving presents twice a year by having their birthday fall on December 25. Among the more well-known are the scientist and mathematician Sir Isaac Newton (1642), the actor Humphrey Bogart (1899), the author Quentin Crisp (1908), the comedian Kenny Everett (1945), the singer Annie Lennox (1954), Shane McGowan of The Pogues (1957), whose name will always be associated with Christmas thanks to his penning of "Fairytale of New York," and the pop star Dido Florian Cloud de Bounevialle Armstrong (1971), better known as just Dido.

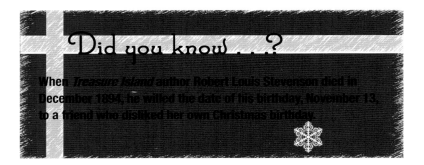

Did you know . . . ?

When *Treasure Island* author Robert Louis Stevenson died in December 1894, he willed the date of his birthday, November 13, to a friend who disliked her own Christmas birthday.

WHY IS TURKEY EATEN AT CHRISTMAS?

What would Christmas dinner be without roast turkey and all the trimmings? (And what would the days following be like without the endless rounds of turkey sandwiches?) But how did this bird become the most intrinsic element of all festive fare?

The turkey originally came from Mexico—not Turkey—and was brought back by Spanish adventurers. The bird was introduced into central Europe by Turkish traders and so became known as the turkey-cock, or simply, turkey. However, just to confuse things even more, the turkey was sometimes known as the Indian peacock (which is even stranger when you consider that India is where the peacock itself originally came from).

This confusion regarding its origins—and hence the bird's name—stemmed from the fact that when Christopher Columbus and his friends first discovered the Americas they were actually looking for an alternative route to India and the East. In their confusion they believed, at first, that they had found India, which is why the West Indies are so named. The first pilgrims indeed found a "great store of wild turkeys" or "Indian peacocks" during the autumn of 1621, famous for the "First Thanksgiving." We don't know for certain, however, that the Pilgrims enjoyed turkey at that harvest feast. This famous bird is now a traditional holiday feast-for-all-occasions.

In other European countries this confusion over the turkey's origins was reflected in its name as well. In France the turkey was called *coq d'Inde* (now corrupted to *dinde*), in Italy it was the *galle d'India*, in Germany its name was *indianische henn*, while throughout the Ottoman Empire it was called the *hindi*.

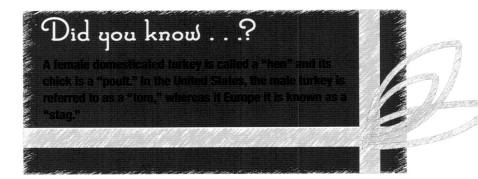

Did you know . . ?

A female domesticated turkey is called a "hen" and its chick is a "poult." In the United States, the male turkey is referred to as a "tom," whereas in Europe it is known as a "stag."

The turkey arrived in England some time after 1510, so it has actually been with us for nearly 500 years. From the sixteenth century, turkeys were reared in Norfolk, which still has strong connections to the bird. For many years the coming of autumn saw an annual migration of turkeys from East Anglia to London, as drovers walked them to market.

Thousands of the birds would be herded in this way. The turkeys averaged only one mile a day, but this would, nonetheless, have soon made them lame—were it not for the fact that to overcome that very problem the farmers tarred their feet or, in some cases, even provided them with little leather boots!

But even before the arrival of the turkey in the British Isles,

poultry was still an important part of the Christmas menu. There were, after all, plenty of native British birds to dine upon, everything from pigeon, plover, and pheasant to capons, woodcock, and swan!

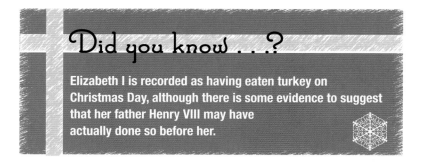

Elizabeth I is recorded as having eaten turkey on Christmas Day, although there is some evidence to suggest that her father Henry VIII may have actually done so before her.

It was the fashionable practice at court to present the birds as if they were still alive, sitting up on the platter as if they were quite happy that they were about to be eaten. To achieve this effect, a bird would be skinned with the utmost care (rather than plucked) before it was cooked. Once the bird had been roasted over the fire, its skin would be replaced and the cuts that had been made to remove it would be sewn up again.

Roast swan was another popular dish among the aristocracy that was presented in this way. There were many different ways of preparing and serving swan. Here is just one of them:

Roast Swan

1 swan
Olive oil

First clean and gut your swan, then cover the outside of the bird with olive oil. Roast it on a spit or, failing that, in the oven. Baste frequently with its own juice and when it is done, carve and serve in pieces. If that's too plain for you, then you can make a Chaudon sauce to accompany the bird, but for this you'll need to have saved the swan's giblets.

Chaudon Sauce

Swan giblets
Red wine vinegar
Broth
Toasted breadcrumbs
Salt
Ginger
Galingale

Start by washing the giblets. While they're still wet, salt them, before placing in a pot. Cover the giblets with water, and boil. Once they're done, drain and cool, before cutting into small pieces. Combine the chopped giblets, breadcrumbs, spices, and broth in a food blender and whizz them up until the whole lot forms a smooth sauce. Bring to a boil in another pan, simmer, and add a little of the red wine vinegar to give it a sharp bite. Serve with the swan.

Before heading off down to the local butcher's to ask for swan, though, you should bear in mind that all swans are protected under the Wildlife and Countryside Act of 1981. The mute swan, however, is even better protected because the species is owned by the Crown, and has been ever since 1482. A small number of shooting licenses are granted to farmers each year, *if* they can prove that swans have damaged their crops, but in all other cases it is an offense to be in possession of a swan carcass, even if the bird died of natural causes!

(In case you're wondering, galingale is another plant of the ginger family.)

The same treatment of dressing the roast bird in its own skin would have been applied to the peacock, another dish that was the preserve of the wealthy. In this case, the bird was presented with its full tail and its head crest and beak covered with gold leaf. A final touch was to put a wick inside the bird's beak which would then be lit just before it was brought to the table. However, some medieval foodies felt that although it was supposed to be a delicacy, the peacock, like so many other wild birds, didn't actually taste that nice. They therefore suggested sewing a roast goose up inside the peacock's skin instead to make the dish more palatable.

Goose was the most popular bird eaten by the smaller households at Christmastime, with chicken and capon popular alternatives. Such domesticated fowl were, of course, more readily available. However, in the north of the country, it wasn't goose but roast beef that was the meat of choice for Christmas dinner.

The Victorians had a goose club, which was a savings club. By saving a little each week you eventually had enough to buy a goose to eat on Christmas Day. In Charles Dickens' *A Christmas Carol*, the Cratchit family were preparing to sit down to enjoy a Christmas goose before Ebenezer Scrooge bought them the best turkey in the shop.

Did you know . . .?

A Christmas Carol wasn't the only festive-themed story penned by Charles Dickens. His other Christmas books include *The Chimes* (1844), *The Cricket on the Hearth* (1845), *The Battle of Life* (1846), and *The Haunted Man and the Ghost's Bargain* (1848).

The growth of industrialized farming has helped to make turkey many people's first choice for Christmas dinner, as it is now very cheap to produce, while the bird itself offers the consumer a large amount of meat for their money. Before the Second World War turkey was still something of a luxury as far as most households were concerned.

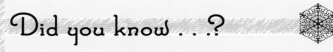

Did you know . . .?

Samuel Pepys, that font of so much seventeenth century social knowledge, wrote of a sauce to accompany turkey, the recipe for which was invented by the then Duke of York (later to become King James II). It was "made from parsley and dry toast beat together in a mortar, together with vinegar, salt and a little pepper," and sounds not unlike a parsley and breadcrumb stuffing.

And what would any roast poultry—whether goose, chicken, turkey, or peacock—be without stuffing? The term "stuffing" didn't appear until 1538; before that time it was called forcemeat and, unsurprisingly, its list of ingredients is slightly different to what we know as stuffing today.

There are some who believe that the recognized antiseptic properties of herbs such as thyme, marjoram, and sage, as used in stuffing, could have helped offset any nasty side effects of eating badly cooked or slightly dodgy poultry. However, there are some more reasons for it having become an important part of the Christmas meal.

Firstly, the addition of stuffing helped to make the meat go further and fill up the stomachs of hungry diners. Secondly, putting the stuffing inside the bird helped it to keep its shape during cooking, and even made it easier for the carcass to stay on the spit while it was being roasted over the fire.

Forcemeat

175 g/6 oz. breadcrumbs	100 g/4 oz. suet
50 g/2 oz. ham (or lean bacon)	1 onion
2 eggs	1 tsp parsley, minced
1 tsp sweet herbs, minced	½ a lemon, rind only
Salt	Cayenne
Pounded mace	Olive oil (or lard)

To make enough forcemeat to accompany one turkey, start by shredding the ham (or bacon); chop the suet with the lemon rind and the herbs, making sure that everything is finely minced. Mince the onion just as finely and add this too. Add some salt, cayenne, and mace, and blend it all together with the breadcrumbs. Take the eggs, beat them and then strain them, and finally mix them with the other ingredients. Shape the forcemeat into balls before frying them in olive oil (or lard, if you're after a more authentic flavor). An alternative to frying is to place the forcemeat balls on a baking tray, before baking them for 30 minutes in a moderate oven.

However, despite the fact that turkey had been on Christmas menus for so long, up until 1851 Queen Victoria still ate swan for Christmas dinner. Then, when she did get turned on to turkey, she (or rather, her cooks) really went to town. The turkey was roasted in a rich pastry and stuffed with . . . three other birds! Inside the turkey was a chicken, inside that was a pheasant, and lastly, inside that, was a woodcock, all with their bones removed—for convenience, of course.

But four birds baked together was nothing compared to the legendary ten-bird roast championed by celebrity chef Hugh Fearnley-Whittingstall. A turkey is stuffed with a goose, duck, mallard, guinea fowl, chicken, pheasant, partridge, pigeon, and woodcock. When cooked it weighs 22 pounds and contains around 10,000 calories (the average turkey contains 3,000 calories). It also takes over nine hours to prepare and cook.

But if all this talk of turkey has got you thinking along the lines of, "What's the perfect way to roast my Christmas turkey this year?" then look no further.

Traditional accompaniments for roast turkey are both cranberry sauce and bread sauce. Cranberry sauce was once restricted to northern rural areas, where wild cranberries grew in abundance. In the south, or the cities, until cranberries became more readily available towards the end of the twentieth century, bread sauce

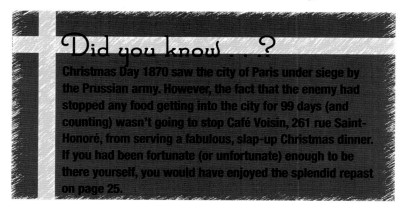

Did you know . . . ?

Christmas Day 1870 saw the city of Paris under siege by the Prussian army. However, the fact that the enemy had stopped any food getting into the city for 99 days (and counting) wasn't going to stop Café Voisin, 261 rue Saint-Honoré, from serving a fabulous, slap-up Christmas dinner. If you had been fortunate (or unfortunate) enough to be there yourself, you would have enjoyed the splendid repast on page 25.

had to suffice. Sausages wrapped in bacon—known by the rather twee term "pigs in blankets"—are also served with the bird.

Christmas Turkey

1 oven-ready turkey
200 g/8 oz. bacon
6 bay leaves

150 g/6 oz. butter
1 lemon
Salt and pepper

Christmas Stuffing

2 large onions
1 tbs dried sage
85 g/3 oz. dried apricots
85 g/3 oz. dried cranberries
900 g/2 lb. pork sausage meat
4 tbs white breadcrumbs
1 egg
Salt and pepper

Preheat the oven to 425°F and while you're doing that, make the stuffing. In a large bowl combine the breadcrumbs with the sage and one of the onions (finely minced), adding a little boiling water before mixing thoroughly. Next in goes the dried fruit; give it another stir. Then add the sausage meat and egg to the mixture, adding a little salt and pepper to taste. Stuff the turkey with the stuffing, pushing it into the neck end and tucking the neck flap back under the turkey. The rest of the stuffing then goes into the body cavity along with one whole, peeled onion. Place the turkey in a deep roasting dish. Smother it with the softened butter combined with the zest of the lemon. Layer the slices of bacon on top, using them to keep the bay leaves next to the skin. When it comes to actually roasting the bird you need to allow 20 minutes per 1 pound, cooking it for another 20 minutes on top of that. A 14 pound bird will feed fourteen people comfortably.

And where did they get all the fresh meat from? Let's just say a trip to the zoo after Christmas would have been a bit of a letdown.

WHERE DOES THE CHRISTMAS TREE COME FROM?

It would be hard to imagine Christmas without the familiar conical form of the festive tree. From December onward (if not before) they can be found everywhere, from homes and schools to department stores and pretty much anywhere people will spend any amount of time during the Christmas period, whether it be a hospital or an office. But where does the tradition come from, and has it always been such an important part of the Christmas celebrations as we know them?

Well, in some ways it is one of the more recently established Christmas traditions, with the decorated tree as we know it rising to popularity during Queen Victoria's reign. And then, in other ways, the tradition is older than Christmas itself. At its root, it's really just another example of an evergreen brought into the home during the cold dark days of winter by our pagan forebears, along with the Yule log, boughs of holly, and mistletoe. But it was actually the Romans who got there first, as they did with so much that has become modern-day Christmas tradition. During the festival of Saturnalia, held in honor of Saturn, the god of agriculture, Ancient Romans decorated trees with small pieces of metal.

The first Christmas trees were decorated with apples, as a symbol of Man's fall in the Garden of Eden when Adam and Eve ate of the fruit of the tree of knowledge. As a result, they were called Paradise trees. In time other decorations were added, in the form of nuts and even red ribbons or strips of paper. Ultimately the apples were replaced by Christmas baubles.

In the Middle Ages, the Paradise tree went up on the feast day dedicated to Adam and Eve, December 24, and to this day, purists believe that you should wait until Christmas Eve to erect your own tree, and then take it down again on Twelfth Night.

Where does the Christmas tree come from? | **27**

Possibly the earliest depiction of a Christmas tree dates from 1521 and comes from Germany. The painting shows a procession of musicians accompanying a horse-riding holy man—who may be a bishop or even Saint Nicholas—parading through a town. One of the men in the procession is holding high a tree decorated with what look like apples.

A candle-lit fir was also erected in a London street in the fifteenth century, but such trees remained as outside decorations and there are no records from the time stating that they were ever taken into the home. Evergreens in other forms were used to decorate houses, though, so it is quite possible that some homes also included a tree, rather than simply being adorned with bits of one.

However, according to some historians, the first recorded mention of an actual Christmas tree appears in a diary from Strasbourg, dated 1605. This particular tree was decorated with paper roses, apples, sweets, and gold foil—the first tinsel.

Did you know . . ?

The people of Latvia like to claim that the first Christmas tree to be erected in public was in their capital city of Riga in 1510. Little is known about the event other than that men in black hats held a ceremony in front of the tree before burning it. Ah yes, the good old traditional Christmas tree-burning ceremony!

In the Church's attempts to Christianize what was essentially a pagan practice, the Christmas fir had Christian symbolism foisted upon it. Since to look at it, its shape was essentially triangular, the three points of the triangle were said to represent the Holy Trinity—God the Father, God the Son, and God the Holy Spirit.

To add weight to the argument that putting up a tree in your house during the winter months was their idea, Christians in the Middle Ages also perpetuated the legend of Saint Boniface, which pre-dated Germanic diary references to Christmas trees by several hundred years. Boniface was a monk (and school-master) from Devon, living in the seventh and eighth centuries, but the event that connects him with the origins of the Christmas tree occurred at Geismar, in Germany. He was there carrying out missionary work, preaching the gospel, at the behest of Pope Gregory II.

The story goes that Boniface came upon a group of pagans worshipping a sacred oak tree. The druids were preparing to sacrifice a baby to their bloodthirsty pagan gods when Saint Boniface came to the infant's rescue. Incensed, he grabbed the axe that was going to be used to end the baby's life and instead laid into the tree, furiously chopping it down. With the babe safe in his arms, he saw that from the roots of the felled oak a fir tree was growing. To his holy eyes the fir was a symbol of Christ's resurrection, with new life growing out of what had been a tree of death.

Sometimes this story is linked to a different saint, the seventh-century Wilfrid of York. In this version the saint set out to cut down an oak tree which was the focus of a druidic cult. As he chopped it down, the oak split and a fir tree grew from its heart. Wilfrid dedicated the fir to Christ, declaring that the evergreen represented the eternal life offered by the Savior.

And then again sixteenth-century folklore states that it was Martin Luther, the German theologian, who was the first person to bring a decorated tree into the home. After walking through a starlit forest of evergreens, Martin felt inspired. Bringing a tree into his own home and illuminating it with candles, he reminded his family that Jesus Christ himself had descended from Heaven to die for our sins. However, there are some historians who claim that there is no evidence of a lighted tree until more than a century after Martin Luther's death in 1546.

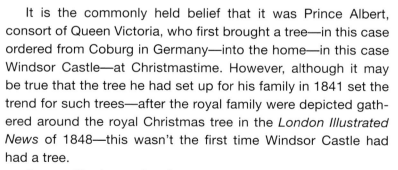

Did you know . . .?

According to the Royal Society for the Prevention of Accidents, there are 1,000 Christmas tree–related emergency room visits every year.

It is the commonly held belief that it was Prince Albert, consort of Queen Victoria, who first brought a tree—in this case ordered from Coburg in Germany—into the home—in this case Windsor Castle—at Christmastime. However, although it may be true that the tree he had set up for his family in 1841 set the trend for such trees—after the royal family were depicted gathered around the royal Christmas tree in the *London Illustrated News* of 1848—this wasn't the first time Windsor Castle had had a tree.

Queen Charlotte, the German consort of King George III and Victoria's grandmother, had ordered a Christmas tree, or *Weihnachtsbaum*, for the Queen's lodge at Windsor in 1800, and trees became a permanent fixture there for a number of years afterwards. The practice had been a common one in Germany, before the royal family popularized it in this country.

Probably the most famous Christmas tree in England is the one given to the city of Westminster by the people of Oslo in Norway. It is a gift given in gratitude for the help Norway received from England during the Second World War when it was occupied by enemy forces. King Haakon of Norway was able to escape to England and set up the Free Norwegian Government. Every year since 1947, the Norwegian tree has been put on display in Trafalgar Square in London. At approximately seventy feet tall, it is the only un-milled tree over twelve feet that is allowed to be imported into the country.

There grows within the grounds of Glastonbury Abbey in Somerset an altogether different kind of Christmas tree. It is a bush of the variety *Crataegus monogyna biflora*, a cultivar of the common hawthorn that flowers twice a year, better known as the Glastonbury Thorn. According to legend, after the death of Christ, Joseph of Arimathea (who gave his tomb for Jesus's body to be interred within) visited England with the intention of spreading the Gospel. While he was visiting the West of England he lay down to rest, but not before thrusting his staff into the ground. When he awoke again he discovered that his staff had miraculously taken root and come into flower.

Did you know . . .?
The first artificial Christmas trees recreated the look of the evergreen fir using goose feathers, dyed green.

From that day, the Glastonbury Thorn has continued to flower on Wearyall Hill every Christmas, a sign of the hope that the birth of the infant Jesus brought to mankind. However, during the seventeenth century and the Puritans' attempted purge of Christmas in all its forms, the original Glastonbury Thorn was uprooted and destroyed. Fortunately, people had been taking cuttings from the holy hawthorn for years and so the tree lived on. It was one of these cuttings that was planted, and subsequently thrived, within the ruins of Glastonbury Abbey, attracting countless visitors over the years.

Just like the Glastonbury Thorn, Christmas trees don't have to be fir trees. In the past, trees such as cherry and common hawthorns have been used, while in India, Christians decorate banana trees at Christmastime. So now the Christmas tree is a part of almost everyone's festive season, whether it be real or fake, with piles of presents beneath and adorned with all manner of decorations, some of them of the edible variety!

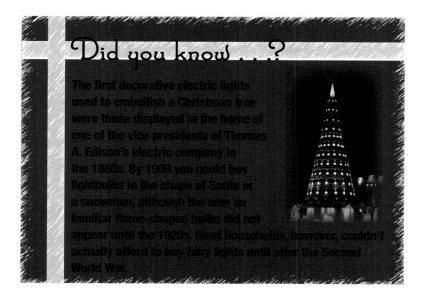

Did you know . . . ?

The first decorative electric lights used to embellish a Christmas tree were those displayed in the home of one of the vice presidents of Thomas A. Edison's electric company in the 1880s. By 1909 you could buy lightbulbs in the shape of Santa or a snowman, although the now so familiar flame-shaped bulbs did not appear until the 1920s. Most households, however, couldn't actually afford to buy fairy lights until after the Second World War.

WHY ARE CARDS SENT AT CHRISTMAS?

For many people, the festive season really gets under way with the sending and receiving of their first Christmas cards, usually some time in November! It's an annual burden, writing endless cards to be sent to people who you last had contact with twelve months before, when you last received a card from them, but it's one that we would not be without.

Because the giving and receiving of cards is so inextricably linked to Christmas, it's hard to imagine a time when we didn't have Christmas cards. But of course something else we take for granted these days is the postal service. Without a postal service there would be no way of sending all those sack loads of cards, and a reliable (and, more importantly, affordable) postal service wasn't created until the mid-1800s. As a result, the greeting card didn't appear until the Victorian era either.

That said, the exchanging of illustrated greetings cards on special occasions itself can be traced back to the Romans and even the Ancient Egyptians before them. Of course, these weren't Christmas cards as we know them, but we came a step closer in the fifteenth century when engravers began printing special Christmas pictures to sell during the festive period. However, these pictures came complete with New Year's greetings rather than Christmas ones. In the Victorian era, it was a popular practice for people to send hand-drawn "Christmas sheets" to their friends and family. These were pictures, on single sheets of paper, with space left for the sender to add his or her name. It also became popular at this time for the more well-to-do members of society to add a printed Christmas message to the calling cards they presented on visiting the house of another well-to-do person.

However, the first true commercial Christmas card—one that we would recognize as being just that—didn't go on sale until 1843. It was printed at the behest of Sir Henry Cole, a businessman and philanthropist. It was Cole who also first came up with the idea of perforated edges for stamps.

Cole commissioned artist John Callcott Horsley to produce the image for the front, which showed a family party, along with vignettes of people carrying out charitable acts for the poor. It also bore the festive message, "A Merry Christmas and a Happy New Year to You!" The black and white card then had to be hand colored. The cards sold for pennies each and Cole managed to shift nearly a thousand of them. The Christmas card had arrived, and it was an instant hit! The Victorians being Victorians, it wasn't long before Christmas cards became more elaborate. Soon there were pop-up cards which opened out into incredible 3D scenes, and ones which implemented cunning techniques to make a character appear to climb out of the card.

By the 1860s, Christmas cards were being mentioned in publications such as *Punch* magazine and the *Times* newspaper. Although they started off with flowery borders and pretty lace edging, soon what we would consider to be more traditional Christmas scenes had begun to appear on the cards. For example, the robin (a perennial favorite) first appeared on a card in 1862.

In 1880, the post office made its first-ever plea to "Post early for Christmas." Nearly ten years prior to this, in 1871, one newspaper complained that the delivery of business mail was being delayed because of the sheer volume of Christmas cards piling up in post offices. By 1873 people had started publishing adverts in newspapers wishing their friends all the very best for the festive season and stating that they would not be sending Christmas cards that year.

Did you know . . .?
Every year, more than 1.8 billion Christmas cards are sent within the United Kingdom. To make all of these cards, over 200,000 trees have to be felled.

WHO IS THE REAL
FATHER CHRISTMAS?

Every Christmas Eve, children the world over await the arrival of one individual more than any other (or at least one of his many lieutenants) with excited anticipation. The image of the jolly old man with his long white beard, red suit, and attendant reindeer couldn't be more familiar, but where did this admittedly peculiar figure come from? Who is, or was, the real Father Christmas? Whether you call him Father Christmas, Santa Claus, Sinterklaus, or Kris Kringle, the semi-historical, semi-legendary figure who inspired the Christmas gift-giver children know and love today was one Saint Nicholas. And he didn't come from the North Pole or Lapland. Saint Nicholas came from Turkey (although, of course, turkeys come from Mexico)!

Did you know . . ?

Santa Claus' official post office is to be found in Rovaniemi, the capital of the Province of Lapland in northern Finland. He receives somewhere in the region of 600,000 letters each year!

Nicholas was the Greek Orthodox Bishop of Myra in fourth-century Byzantine Anatolia. His parents both died when he was still a young man, leaving him a considerable fortune. Shunning his wealth and privileged background to join the Church, Nicholas then made it his mission to give his riches away to those more deserving, and in greater need, than he. The best-known example of his charity is the one which led to children hanging up their stockings on Christmas Eve for Santa to fill with gifts (see page 62).

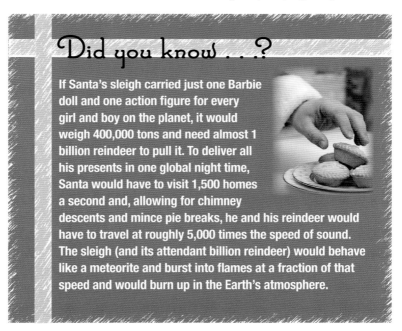

Did you know . . .?

If Santa's sleigh carried just one Barbie doll and one action figure for every girl and boy on the planet, it would weigh 400,000 tons and need almost 1 billion reindeer to pull it. To deliver all his presents in one global night time, Santa would have to visit 1,500 homes a second and, allowing for chimney descents and mince pie breaks, he and his reindeer would have to travel at roughly 5,000 times the speed of sound. The sleigh (and its attendant billion reindeer) would behave like a meteorite and burst into flames at a fraction of that speed and would burn up in the Earth's atmosphere.

Nicholas is credited with performing various miracles during his lifetime, which have led to him becoming the patron saint of many different groups of people. A number of legends tell of how he saved ships and their crews when threatened by storms at sea. As a result he is the patron saint of sailors.

He is also the patron of children. This may be thanks to another story told about him: the miracle of the boys in a barrel. In some versions of the story there are two boys, in others three, but the rest of the details are roughly the same. The story goes that two boys were travelling to Athens, where they were to be educated, but had been told by their father to stop off at Myra on the way to receive the bishop's blessing. When they arrived at the town, night had already fallen and so they took a room at a local inn, intending to visit Nicholas the next morning.

Unfortunately for the boys, the innkeeper decided to rob them, thinking that their possessions would make easy pickings. That night the felon crept into the room where they slept and murdered them where they lay. To hide his heinous crime, and profit still further from the villainous deed, he chopped up their bodies, pickling them in barrels of brine, planning to sell their flesh to his customers as salted pork.

However, Bishop Nicholas learnt that the boys were due to visit him and so set out in search of them. His enquiries eventually brought him to the inn and, when questioned about the boys, the innkeeper panicked, telling Nicholas that the boys had been there but had left the following morning. Nicholas was having none of it and set about searching the premises. It did not take him long to find the barrels which held the boys' dismembered corpses.

With a dramatic change of heart, no doubt brought on by extreme guilt, the innkeeper broke down and confessed his sins, begging the bishop for forgiveness. The saint was utterly convinced by the innkeeper's desire to repent and prayed for both him, and the dead boys. As he concluded his prayer, the body parts reunited and the boys emerged from the brine barrels, alive and wholly intact. And so they continued on their way to Athens.

This highly venerated bishop died on December 6 in either AD 326, 345, or 352 (historians aren't certain). As a result, December 6 is his feast day and in some countries it is after sunset on that day that Father Christmas visits children to bestow his gifts.

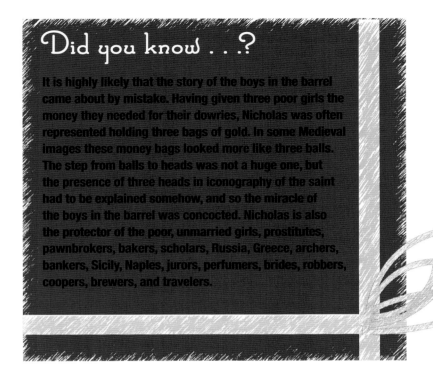

One of the first places to benefit from gifts brought by the saint was the town of Bari in Italy. Pilgrims were big business in the Middle Ages and to attract them a place needed relics,

ideally something associated with Christ but, failing that, the earthly remains of a popular saint.

In 1097, Norman pirates raided Myra and stole Saint Nicholas' remains from his tomb. The raiders claimed that they were saving the saint from the advancing Muslims but it is more than likely that they were actually motivated by a desire to ensure Bari's future prosperity.

Did you know . . .?

During the thirteenth and fourteenth centuries, it was the custom within the great cathedrals to appoint a boy bishop from among the choristers on the feast of Saint Nicholas. Wearing full Episcopal garb—miter and crosier included—his term of office lasted from December 6 until Holy Innocents' Day, December 28. During this time the boy bishop carried out all the functions of a priest, from taking church services to appointing canons (from among his fellow choristers). This practice began to die out in Tudor times, when both Henry VIII and Elizabeth I tried to ban the potentially blasphemous tradition.

But the image we now have of Father Christmas has its origins in more than just the legendary life of one particular saint. In truth, Father Christmas' origins go back much further than fourth-century Turkey. For the Norsemen of Scandinavia, the season of Yule was as much a dark time ruled over by demons and malevolent spirits. It was best to stay indoors, to escape the baleful gaze of the nocturnal flyer Odin. Odin also brought winter to the world. In this guise he was accompanied by his Dark Helper, a demonic horned creature who punished wrong-doers. This figure would resurface later as Father Christmas' assistant.

Thor, the Norse god of thunder, may well have had a hand in influencing the development of the Father Christmas myth, for he rode across the sky in an iron chariot pulled by two huge goats, called Tanngrisnir and Tanngnjóstr (in English, Gnasher and Cracker), rather like Santa's sleigh with its team of reindeer. There is also evidence that pagan peoples once worshipped an elemental spirit called Old Man Winter. He too went into the mix that was to eventually produce the figure of Father Christmas.

Christmas itself has been personified for centuries within the British Isles. In a carol, the words of which were written around the year 1500, he is called "Sir Christèmas."

"*Nowell, nowell, nowell, nowell.*"
"Who is there that singeth so, *nowell, nowell, nowell*?"
"I am here, Sir Christèmas."
"Welcome, my lord Sir Christèmas!
Welcome to all, both more and less,
Come near, *nowell.*"
"*Dieu vous garde, beaux sieurs*, tidings I you bring:
A maid hath borne a child full young,
Which causeth you to sing*, nowell.*"
"Christ is now born of a pure maid, born of a pure maid;
In an ox stall he is laid,
Wherefore sing we at a brayed, *nowell.*"
"*Buvez bien, buvez bien par toute la compagnie.*
Make good cheer and be right merry,
And sing with us now joyfully*, nowell!*"

To the Medieval mind there had to be balance in all things. Just as there was Heaven and Hell, rich and poor, Father Christmas couldn't just give to the good and let those who had been bad get off scot-free. And so the character of the Dark Helper reemerged. Sometimes called Black Peter, under the influence of the Church, the Dark Helper became a demon enslaved by the saint.

As well as having horns, he was covered in shaggy black hair, and carried a birch rod with which he would punish naughty children and also badly behaved women! Black Peter is known by different names across Europe, but his purpose remains the same: to be the antithesis of Father Christmas. To some he is Krampus (from the Old German word *krampen*, meaning "claw"), Pelz Nickel, or Klaubauf. To others he is Knecht Reprechte, dressed in animal skins and straw, or even Old Nick, the Devil himself! People living in the seventeenth century had a different concept of a "Father Christmas," but he was a figure that oversaw the community celebrations rather than someone who gave presents to children. The modern image we now have of Father Christmas didn't really develop until well into the nineteenth century. Up until that time he had been everything from slim to fat, tall to tiny, elfin, troll-like, a pagan druid, a variation on the spirit of nature in the form of the Green Man (bedecked with garlands of holly, ivy and mistletoe), a drunk (riding in a sleigh pulled by turkeys), and the jolly and generous Lord Christmas.

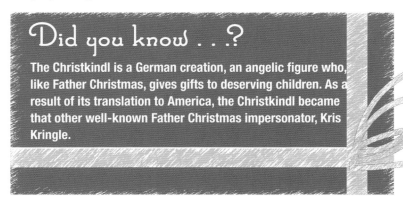

Did you know . . .?

The Christkindl is a German creation, an angelic figure who, like Father Christmas, gives gifts to deserving children. As a result of its translation to America, the Christkindl became that other well-known Father Christmas impersonator, Kris Kringle.

It was Clement Clarke Moore (1779–1863), the American Episcopalian minister and author of the poem "An Account of a Visit from Saint Nicholas" (better known by its first line, "'Twas the Night Before Christmas"), who introduced the team of eight reindeer and had Santa gaining entry to the house down the chimney. In fact, American culture has had a huge impact on the development of the modern image of Santa Claus, which originally came to the United States from the Netherlands in the guise of Sinterklaus. The German American caricaturist Thomas Nast also had his part to play in creating what we would now call the traditional image of Santa Claus. His classic version of the jolly fellow appeared in

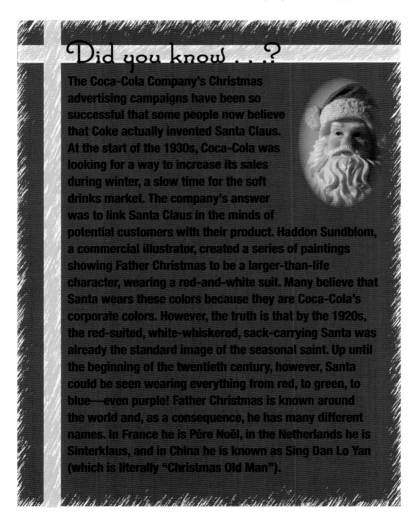

Did you know . . .?

The Coca-Cola Company's Christmas advertising campaigns have been so successful that some people now believe that Coke actually invented Santa Claus. At the start of the 1930s, Coca-Cola was looking for a way to increase its sales during winter, a slow time for the soft drinks market. The company's answer was to link Santa Claus in the minds of potential customers with their product. Haddon Sundblom, a commercial illustrator, created a series of paintings showing Father Christmas to be a larger-than-life character, wearing a red-and-white suit. Many believe that Santa wears these colors because they are Coca-Cola's corporate colors. However, the truth is that by the 1920s, the red-suited, white-whiskered, sack-carrying Santa was already the standard image of the seasonal saint. Up until the beginning of the twentieth century, however, Santa could be seen wearing everything from red, to green, to blue—even purple! Father Christmas is known around the world and, as a consequence, he has many different names. In France he is Père Noël, in the Netherlands he is Sinterklaus, and in China he is known as Sing Dan Lo Yan (which is literally "Christmas Old Man").

Harper's Weekly, in 1863. Before then, most depictions of Santa had shown him as a tall, thin man. However, Nast drew him as the bearded, plump individual known today. So, the Father Christmas—Santa Claus, Kris Kringle, call him what you like—that we know and love today is really an amalgamation of the gift-giving Santa Claus, the personification of the festive season Father Christmas, and a fourth-century Turkish saint.

Although the idea of a beneficent bringer of gifts at Christmastime is almost universal in Christian countries the world over, it isn't always Santa Claus who does the honors. In Spain and South America it is the Three Kings who bring presents, just as they gave gifts to the Christ child. In Italy a kindly old witch called La Befana gives children sweets if they've been good and a piece of coal if they haven't. In Russia it is either the grandmotherly Babouschka or Grandfather Frost, while in Scandinavia (for many the home of Santa Claus) gift giving is the job of a tribe of gnomes, one of whom goes by the name of Julenissen.

Did you know . . .?

According to the Italian legend of La Befana, the three wise men stopped at her home on their way to pay homage to the Christ child, and invited her to go with them. But La Befana had lost her own child to plague and found the prospect of seeing another baby too upsetting. But after the wise men had left she changed her mind. She set off in pursuit on her broomstick (as you do when you're a witch) but never found the Magi again. Instead, every time she came across a good child's stocking she filled it with toys and sweets in an effort to make up for her foolishness.

WHY ARE CAROLS SUNG
AT CHRISTMASTIME?

Carol-singing as we would recognize it dates back to at least the thirteenth century in England, although we might not recognize many of the actual carols from that time. The idea of caroling is now inextricably tied to Christmas, but it should be remembered that carols have been written for many other festivals that occur throughout the year. A song does not even have to have any religious relevance for it to be called a carol. The word *carol* comes from the Greek *choros*, meaning "a dance," via the Latin *choraula* and the French *carole*, which was specifically a ring-dance. The English spelling of "carol" is first seen in the *Cursor Mundi* dating from around 1300. In this context, a carol was described as "a ring-dance in which the dancers themselves sing the governing music."

It is hard to pin down exactly what a carol is—beyond the connection to dancing, although this itself does not really apply to many carols anymore—as the word has been used to refer to such widely varying pieces of music, from ones connected to the Nativity to jovial drinking songs. Although most would now agree that a carol is a Christmas song with connections either to the religious side or the pagan aspects of the midwinter festival, at one time such forms of music were condemned by the Church.

The earliest known hymn in honor of the Nativity is "*Jesus refulsit omnium*" (meaning "Jesus, Light of all the Nations"). It was written by Saint Hilary of Poitiers who died in AD 368. Nativity hymns such as this were solemn affairs and strictly religious. Something more like the carols we know today developed in

Italy among the followers of Saint Francis of Assisi. Having spent much of his youth as a troubadour, Francis decided that the best way to teach people about Jesus Christ was through song. Francis, and the community of friars he founded, set about writing what many consider to be the first true Christmas carols.

Some of them were performed around a Nativity scene that Saint Francis set up one Christmas Eve. In 1224, Franciscans brought the carols to England and began to compose new ones in English. The earliest surviving such carol we have written at that time is "A Child is Boren Amonges Man." In thirteenth-century England, carols were sung in respectful imitation of the angels who, according to the Gospel writers, sang *"Gloria in excelsis Deo"* at Christ's birth. At that time, these religious songs were sung only by the priests and choristers in church. However, the lyrical content of some carols often incorporated older pagan customs. One such example is the "Boar's Head Carol." Others are those about the holly and the ivy, with all their pagan symbolism intact.

The carol also developed hand-in-hand with the mystery play. The "Coventry Carol" was itself written for one such play, special to the city of Coventry. Some carols were effectively sung narrative poems, such as the "Cherry Tree Carol," while others interspersed the ballad structure with lines of Latin that all regular church-goers would recognize, even if they didn't actually understand what they meant, as in *In dulce jubilo*. (This style is commonplace in many early sixteenth century carols.)

The earliest printed collection of carols was produced by William Caxton's apprentice, and eventual successor, Wynkyn de Worde, in 1521. Richard Kele's *Christmas Carols Newly Imprinted* appeared in 1550, but this particular collection already suffered from the moralizing influence of the growing Puritan movement. During the sixteenth and seventeenth centuries, the Puritans made it their mission to take much of the fun out of the festive repertoire. They saw the Christian festival of Christmas as having been corrupted by the more immoral, secular celebrations associated with the season. And they were successful, for a while, too.

As a result, the Puritans did much to put paid to the singing of carols for a good few years. This temporary suppression of the carol was partly as a result of its association with dancing. Where worship out of doors had been perfectly acceptable in the past, the Puritans restrained their worship to the meeting house.

Likewise there was no movement allowed within church services; even processions conducted as part of the Sunday service had been removed.

The Puritans also had it in for the mystery plays, for which many of the earlier carols had been written. They did not consider it appropriate to re-enact such holy scenes as Christ's birth, and so in 1642 an "Order for Stage Plays to Cease" was passed. Songs that suffered as a consequence included the fifteenth-century "Salutation Carol" and the even earlier *"Angelus ad Virginem,"* which dated from the middle of the thirteenth century.

Many carols contained the relics of a more superstitious age, such as "The Holly and the Ivy," which the Puritans could not tolerate. Only material from the scriptures was considered suitable to be used in songs of worship, so out went such legendary carols as "The Carnal and the Crane" and "King Herod and the Cock." However, under Puritan rule the carol did not vanish altogether. As long as the songs were holy and somber affairs, sung with all due reverence, they were acceptable. 1642 saw a collection called *Good and True, Fresh and New Christmas Carols* published, while after the Restoration other collections such as *New Carols for this Merry Time of Christmas* (1661) and *New Christmas Carols* (1662) followed. By writing their own carols— although they were not what the Medieval merry-makers would have called a carol—the Puritans hoped to convert people to their way of thinking. Nonetheless, many of the carols written at this time are no longer in use today, and with good reason. The majority of them were intended to correct people and improve their lives. Such penitential pieces did not prove very popular. One that has endured, however, is the lullaby "Wither's Rocking Hymn," written by staunch Puritan George Wither (1588–1667).

Although Christmas carols did not enjoy a massive revival after the Restoration of the monarchy in 1660, at the turn of the eighteenth century new carols were being written. "While Shepherds Watched" and "Hark! The Herald Angels Sing" are both from this time. It could be argued that these were not really Christmas carols but Christmas hymns, as were what came after, since the music was no longer suggestive of dancing, whereas "I Saw Three Ships" (which dates from the Middle Ages) has a galloping rhythm that would have suited a ring-dance very well. It wasn't until the mid-nineteenth century, though, that the carol, along with the rest of Christmas, enjoyed a more substantial revival, and yet even then, at the beginning, it was mainly thanks to two men in particular.

The Reverend John Mason Neale was the Warden of Sackville College, East Grinstead, in Sussex, and a known translator of Greek and Latin hymns. The Reverend Thomas Helmore was Vice-Principal of St Mark's College, Chelsea, and an accomplished musician. These two clergymen worked together on translating and interpreting the sixteenth-century tunes found inside what was possibly the only surviving copy of an ancient book called

the *Piae Cantiones*, compiled by one Theodoricus Petrus of Nyland, Finland, in 1582. In 1853, Neale and Helmore published the fruits of their labors in a collection of twelve carols under the title *Carols for Christmas-tide*. The carol "Unto Us a Boy Is Born" has been passed on to us from this collection (although it can also be found in a fifteenth-century manuscript), as has "Good King Wenceslas."

Seeing the success of Neale and Helmore's work, and the passion with which it was received, others soon followed in their footsteps, bringing out their own carol collections. Many of those sung

today were written at the end of the nineteenth century and the beginning of the twentieth. "See Amid the Winter's Snow," "Once in Royal David's City," "In the Bleak Midwinter," and even "Away in a Manger" were all written at this time.

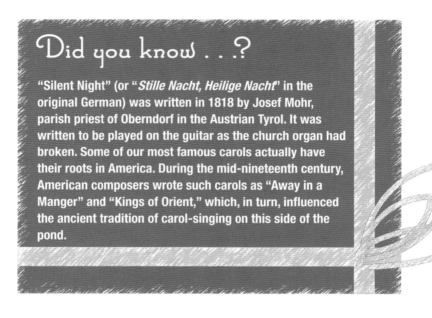

Did you know . . .?

"Silent Night" (or "*Stille Nacht, Heilige Nacht*" in the original German) was written in 1818 by Josef Mohr, parish priest of Oberndorf in the Austrian Tyrol. It was written to be played on the guitar as the church organ had broken. Some of our most famous carols actually have their roots in America. During the mid-nineteenth century, American composers wrote such carols as "Away in a Manger" and "Kings of Orient," which, in turn, influenced the ancient tradition of carol-singing on this side of the pond.

Carol-singing itself enjoyed a revival during the Victorian era. The long-lasting impact of the Puritans on Christmas meant that carols were not really sung in church again until the 1880s. It was then that the familiar service of nine lessons and carols was drawn up by the Bishop of Truro, E.W. Benson, who later went on to become Archbishop of Canterbury.

New carols are still being written today, of course (along with endless festive pop ditties), but it is the carols of the late nineteenth century and those that have made it to us from the sixteenth century that are sung every Christmas with the greatest fondness and fervor.

Did you know . . .?

The name Bethlehem, as in the carol "O, Little Town of Bethlehem" and Jesus' birthplace, is an Arabic word meaning "house of bread."

WHY DO PEOPLE OPEN ADVENT CALENDARS IN THE RUN-UP TO CHRISTMAS?

The period of four weeks leading up to Christmas is called Advent, from the Latin *adveneo* meaning "to come." In this context it refers to the coming of Jesus, and so in the Christian Church it has always been a time of preparation, in expectation of the Feast of the Nativity.

In many households the days left until Christmas are counted down with the aid of an Advent calendar. From December 1 onwards, one numbered door or window is opened to reveal the image—and now, more often than not, the chocolate—hidden behind it. It used to be the case that the last window was for December 24, which had an image of the Nativity behind it, but now calendars can last as far as the New Year! It is easy to see how the season of Advent came about in the early Church, but what of the calendars used to count down the days to Christmas? The first Advent calendars, as we would recognize them, were made in the middle of the nineteenth century.

Even before that, however, German Lutherans were already marking off the days of Advent by some physical means, as they had done since at least the beginning of the century. In some households this meant lighting a new candle each day or hanging up a religious image, but it could be something as simple (and cost-free) as marking a line in chalk on the door of the house. If candles were used, they were mounted on a device called an Advent clock. The first recognizable Advent calendar, however, didn't appear until 1851, and even then it was a handmade creation. There is some debate as to when the first printed calendar appeared. Some say that it was produced in 1902 or 1903, in Hamburg, Germany; others claim that it did not appear until 1908, and that it was the creation of one Gerhard Lang, a printer from Munich.

Lang's calendar was certainly the basis of our modern Advent calendars. His first efforts were made up of twenty-four tiny, colored pictures that had to be stuck onto a piece of cardboard. In the years to come, however, he was to introduce the doors that are so integral to Advent calendars today.

During the Second World War, the manufacture of Advent calendars ceased, as cardboard was rationed. However, once the war was over, the firm of Richard Sellmer Verlag began producing

them once more, and was almost wholly responsible for their widespread popularity.

Although it might seem like a more recent addition, Advent calendars replete with chocolate treats have actually been around for at least half a century, and were certainly available by 1958. Advent calendars are no longer made only of card either. Cloth versions, with pockets in place of doors to open, are popular, as are strings of stockings which have to be filled with toys and gifts for the child by a benevolent parent. And then there are the true twenty-first-century Advent calendars that can be "opened" and viewed online.

However, in Germany, the spiritual home of the Advent calendar, certain towns go that extra mile. The Rathaus of Gengenbach, a town located within Germany's Black Forest, is turned into a gigantic Advent calendar every year, thanks to the fact that it conveniently has twenty-four main windows. Starting on the evening of November 30, each of these windows is unveiled in turn to reveal a festive scene. In the town of Reith, each of the twenty-four windows is actually located in a different building and collectively referred to as the town's walking Advent calendar, while in Dresden the city's Advent calendar is constructed at the site of its Christmas market, in the Striezelmarkt, in the form of a fairytale castle.

Christmas Greetings

WHY ARE STOCKINGS HUNG UP ON CHRISTMAS EVE?

I t has long been the practice that on Christmas Eve, children (and sometimes optimistic adults) hang stockings by the fire, or at the foot of their bed, in the hope that Father Christmas will deposit presents for them to open on Christmas morning. Nowadays, of course, pillow cases have become a popular alternative. In Clement Clarke Moore's popular poem, "An Account of a Visit from Saint Nicholas," we are told that:

> The stockings were hung by the chimney with care,
> In the hope that St Nicholas would soon be there. . . .

And indeed, this tradition has its origins in one of the myths surrounding the original Santa Claus himself, Saint Nicholas.

The legend can be traced back to the eighth century and involves a father and his three daughters. This family had fallen on hard times and could no longer afford even the basics, such as food and clothing. There was certainly no way that the poor man could afford the dowries that the girls would need to get married. Faced with such a dire predicament, the girls' father decided that the only option left open to them, to save them from starvation, was for the girls to enter into the world's oldest profession.

One night, however, Saint Nicholas happened to be passing the house where the family lived and he heard the father and his daughters bemoaning their desperate situation. Nicholas had been left a considerable fortune by his parents, but now there were only three bags of gold left. No matter—it was enough to help the distraught spinsters.

Having collected the cash from his home, Nicholas returned later that night. One by one he dropped the bags of gold down the chimney, where they landed in the girls' stockings that had been hung up to dry in front of the fire. And so, the daughters were saved from a life of iniquity and poverty.

In some versions of the story Nicholas threw the bags of gold in through a window, as each of the girls came to marriageable age, and in others the gold drops down the chimney to land in the girls' shoes, rather than their stockings. But the sentiment is the same in all of them, with Saint Nicholas cast in the role of the generous, yet secretive benefactor.

Although it is difficult to determine when the practice of hanging up stockings specifically to receive presents from Saint Nicholas began, we do know that it was so popular by the early seventeenth century that one Protestant priest complained about parents telling their children that Saint Nicholas had brought them their presents, as it was "a bad custom, because it points children to the saint, while yet we know that not Saint Nicholas but the holy Christ Child gives us all good things for body and soul. . . . "

The three bags of gold with which the saint saved the poor girls' reputations has survived to this day in another, rather more surprising form. A symbol of giving, the three bags of gold, have become the three balls on the traditional pawnbroker's sign. This dates from the Middle Ages, and Lombard Street in London. At this time, the area became home to many pawnbrokers who, when searching for a symbol to represent their trade, had to look no further than the Church of Saint Nicholas, which stood in Lombard Street itself. The statue of the saint on top of the church was shown holding the familiar money bags, which Medieval artists had painted as being round, and so they appeared as balls. This symbol of the three bags of gold was then adopted by the pawnbrokers' businesses and has remained associated with them ever since.

As a consequence, the hanging out of stockings on Christmas Eve is one of the older traditions that have become linked to the modern commercial Christmas. Nowadays many people seem to have forgotten that once upon a time Santa delivered presents only to those deserving of such generosity as a result of their own good behavior during the previous year.

Did you know . . .?

It is traditional among many families for each child to receive a tangerine in their stocking, along with all their other presents. One of the oldest varieties is the Dancy tangerine, which has a loose, pliable peel. The tangerine used to be considered an exotic fruit and, as it was available only in December, it made the perfect Christmas treat for children to receive from Father Christmas. There is also a legend that the tradition was started by twelfth-century French nuns who left socks full of fruit, nuts, and tangerines at the houses of the poor.

WHY DO PEOPLE PUT UP CHRISTMAS DECORATIONS?

Happy Christmas to Yo

People have always festooned their homes with some manner of decorations, whether boughs of winter greenery or with enough electric lights to double their energy bills for the year. But where did it all start? Our Norse ancestors used evergreens—mainly holly, ivy, mistletoe, and the branches of fir trees—to decorate their homes during the winter months, and to remind people that life would return to the world again. In time, other man-made decorations, such as bows of red ribbon and lit candles, would be added to enhance what nature had already provided.

With the growth of towns and cities, by the late nineteenth century it was not so easy for some people to simply take a stroll through the nearest stretch of woodland to collect their winter greenery, and so it was that commercialism played its hand; someone had to bring to market for the urban masses what had once been free to all.

This is the case now, of course, more than ever before. Much of the mistletoe that goes into decorating our homes at Christmastime, for example, is actually harvested from apple orchards in France. Following the example set by Queen Victoria and Prince Albert in the 1840s, the trend of having a Christmas tree in the home grew during the nineteenth century, and so the demand increased to have things to put on it.

Did you know . . .?

Before the advent of fairy lights, many people lit up their Christmas trees with lighted candles. However, for most people, beeswax candles were beyond their budget. As a cheaper alternative they burned tallow candles. These were made from animal fat and so would have added a distinct aroma all of their own and a good deal of smoke to the festive home.

Why do people put up Christmas decorations? | **67**

Other than lit candles, of one form or another, at first many Christmas tree decorations were of an edible nature. There were sweets, fruit, and even wafers; then came small presents and paper ornaments. By the 1880s glass ornaments were all the rage, with baubles replacing the once traditional apples hung on the old-fashioned Paradise tree (a precursor to the modern Christmas tree)—a reminder of the forbidden fruit tasted by Adam and Eve in the Garden of Eden.

And now we have strings of fairy lights, tinsel by the yard, and all manner of decorations with which to adorn our homes. Then there is the belief that it is unlucky to leave Christmas decorations up after Twelfth Night. But why should this be the case? Druidic beliefs held that wood spirits were in the evergreens brought into the home, and that they could cause mischief in the household. However, they were prevented from doing so during the period lasting from Christmas Eve to Twelfth Night. After that they were free to do their worst again.

Long after the original pagan rituals and traditions had been replaced or amalgamated with Christian flavored versions, in the Middle Ages people found it hard to shake off their devotedly held superstitious beliefs so easily. Common folklore still said that the leafy boughs brought into the home at Christmastime were verily budding with nature spirits which could cause mischief if they weren't handled properly. And the superstition has lasted to this day, even though the reasons for this have in most cases long been forgotten. If you fancy making some of your own edible tree decorations, as your forebears once did, why not try this recipe for cinnamon and ginger biscuits?

Roll the dough out flat, and fairly thin, before cutting it into the shapes you desire. There are plenty of seasonal biscuit cutters that are ideal for this job. Just remember, the less complicated

Cinnamon and Ginger Biscuit Decorations

100 g/4 oz. caster sugar
100 g/4 oz. unsalted butter
200 g/8 oz. plain flour, sifted
1 tsp of ground ginger
½ tsp of cinnamon
½ tsp of vanilla extract
1 small egg, beaten
Thin, red ribbon or gold cord

To make the biscuits, start by creaming the sugar and butter together in a bowl, then add the egg. Sift the flour into the bowl and stir it in along with the cinnamon and ginger. Add the vanilla extract. Mix all of this together until a firm dough is produced. Ideally you want to leave the dough in the fridge for 1 to 2 hours at this point, but you can get away without doing so if time's not on your side.

the shape, the less likely it is to crumble and break, and so will survive the ultimate transition to your Christmas tree. Pierce the unbaked biscuit with a knitting needle or skewer to make a hole through which to thread the ribbon later.

Grease and flour a baking sheet and preheat the oven to 375°F. Place the biscuit shapes onto the sheet and cook at the top of the oven for 10 minutes. Once they're done, leave them on the baking sheet for a few minutes before transferring them to a wire rack to finish cooling. Thread a length of the ribbon or cord through the hole in each biscuit and tie it to form a loop, so you can hang them up. If you want, you can decorate the biscuits before hanging them on your tree; you could use white icing or melted chocolate and then embellish your miniature master-pieces with silver balls, or chopped nuts and glacé cherries. And you're done. Just don't expect these decorations to last until Twelfth Night!

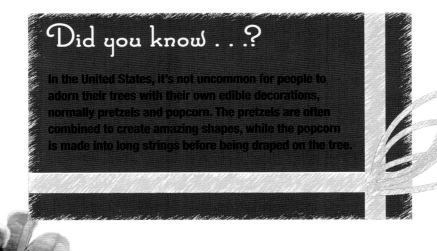

Did you know . . .?

In the United States, it's not uncommon for people to adorn their trees with their own edible decorations, normally pretzels and popcorn. The pretzels are often combined to create amazing shapes, while the popcorn is made into long strings before being draped on the tree.

WHAT IS FIGGY
PUDDING?

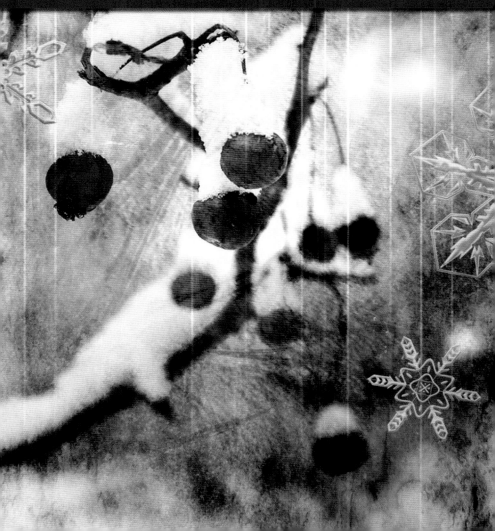

Let's get one thing clear from the start: figgy pudding is not Christmas pudding. That's plum pudding. The constituent ingredient of figgy pudding is figs, whereas plum pudding—the traditional Christmas pudding—should be made with plums. Easy, isn't it? So, in that case, why is everyone so familiar with figgy pudding when it's hardly eaten anymore? Well, it's all down to the carol "We Wish You a Merry Christmas" in which the name of the pudding is mentioned:

Oh, bring us a figgy pudding;
Oh, bring us a figgy pudding;
Oh, bring us a figgy pudding and a cup of good cheer.
We won't go until we get some;
We won't go until we get some;
We won't go until we get some, so bring some out here.

Many people would be surprised by the appearance of figgy pudding, which looks like a white Christmas pudding. The following recipe for figgy pudding serves four.

Today's traditional Christmas pudding, like so much of our modern Christmas, comes from the Victorian era. However, long before anyone ate Christmas pudding of any description, people living during the Medieval period would have tucked into a hearty bowl of frumenty—that's a spicy porridge-like dish made with almond milk, to you and me. The following recipe dates from the fifteenth century.

Figgy Pudding

280 ml/½ pt. of milk

175 g/6 oz. dried figs

100 g/4 oz. suet

75 g/3 oz. raisins (or sultanas)

50 g/2 oz. dates

1 tbs of honey

½ tsp of ground cinnamon

¼ tsp of ginger

200 g/8 oz. flour

140 ml/¼ pt. of brandy

100 g/4 oz. prunes

50 g/2 oz. dried apricots

25 g/1 oz. dried apples

½ tsp grated lemon peel

¼ tsp of ground nutmeg

Whipped cream

This dish needs a little preparation time. The day before you plan to make the figgy pudding, soak the prunes, apricots, and apples in water, and soak the raisins (or sultanas) in the brandy. Then before you prepare the dish, remove the stones from the prunes and the figs.

Now we come to the making of the pudding itself. Sift the flour into a mixing bowl, stir in the suet and mix together with cold water until a soft dough is formed. Turn the dough out onto a floured board and knead it until smooth. Grease a large pudding basin and roll out two-thirds of the pastry to line it.

Melt the honey and stir in the grated lemon peel, cinnamon, nutmeg, and ginger, then add this to the soaked fruits and brandy mixture. Mix well and then place inside the pastry-lined bowl. Moisten the edges of the pastry with water and cover with a lid rolled out from the rest of the pastry. Press the edges together to seal it. Cover the lot with greased greaseproof paper (or aluminum foil) and steam for two hours, topping up the boiling water from time to time to ensure that it doesn't evaporate. To serve, turn out onto a plate and serve with the whipped cream.

Frumenty

250 g/10 oz. cracked wheat
5 cups of water
1 cup of beef stock
1 cup of almond milk
2 beaten egg yolks
A pinch of dried saffron threads
A pinch of salt

Boil the wheat in the water until it's softened (which should take about 15 minutes) and then remove it from the heat, leaving it to stand so that the rest of the water is absorbed. Add the beef stock and the almond milk, and bring it back to a boil, before reducing the heat to a low setting. Stir the mixture for approximately 5 minutes. Stir in the beaten egg yolks and saffron, and keep stirring until the egg starts to thicken. It is important not to let the mixture boil. Take it off the heat and let it stand for another 5 minutes (during which time the mixture will continue to thicken) before serving.

If you don't want to go to the trouble of making almond milk you can simply substitute it with ordinary milk. But if you do fancy the idea of making almond milk for yourself, here's how to do it.

Almond Milk

100 g/4 oz. blanched almonds
1–2 tbs of ice water
1 cup of boiling water

Grind the almonds with the ice water in a mortar (or put them in a blender). Put the resulting paste into a bowl, adding the boiling water. Allow the mixture to stand for 15 minutes before straining it through a metal sieve. The resulting almond milk will last for three days if kept refrigerated. Frumenty was eaten as an accompaniment to meat, traditionally venison, and was also served up with porpoise! As well as being a popular part of the traditional Celtic Christmas meal, it was also eaten on Mother's Day, when the inclusion of eggs would have provided a brief respite from the traditional Lenten fast.

Although the idea of eating porridge on Christmas day might seem a little strange to us now, in areas of Scandinavia it's still part of Christmas dinner. By Tudor times, people had graduated from eating spiced porridge to consuming Christmas puddings which—rather like mince pies—contained more than just the dried fruit and spices we're familiar with today. A typical Tudor pudding would contain meat as well as oatmeal and spices. The preferred method of cooking this little lot was to boil it, and to stop the pudding falling apart in the bubbling vat it was stuffed into a pig's intestine first, rather like sausages are today. In fact the pudding ended up looking like a fat sausage and would be served by the slice. But another hundred years later and the list of ingredients had changed again. If one recipe for Christmas pudding can be considered more traditional than any other, then it is probably that enjoyed by the Pudding King himself, George I.

King George I's Christmas Pudding (1714)

10 eggs	680 g/1½ lb. shredded suet
450 g/1 lb. dried plums	450 g/1 lb. raisins
450 g/1 lb. mixed peel	450 g/1 lb. currants
450 g/1 lb. sultanas	450 g/1 lb. flour
450 g/1 lb. sugar	450 g/1 lb. breadcrumbs
1 tsp mixed spice	1 tsp grated nutmeg
280 ml/½ pt. of milk	½ tsp of salt
The juice of a lemon	A large glass of brandy

Having mixed up all of the ingredients, let the whole lot stand for 12 hours before boiling the mixture for 8 hours. Come Christmas Day you boil it again for 2 hours. This list of ingredients above will produce about 9 lbs of pudding.

An alternative recipe for a rather more alcoholic plum pudding comes from the Edwardians, who are known for being just as wildly excessive as people are today.

Plum Pudding (1909)

1 kg/2¼ lbs raisins
1 kg/2¼ lbs currants
175 g/6 oz. finely chopped candied peel
13 eggs
850 ml/1½ pts of milk
1½ cups of breadcrumbs
680 g/1½ lbs flour
680 g/1½ lbs finely chopped suet
3 wineglasses of brandy
2 wineglasses of rum

Mix the ingredients together well and then spread between two buttered basins, to make two large puddings. Boil them for 14 hours. Halfway between frumenty and plum pudding is a concoction called plum porridge. Plum porridge was made with meat broth, thickened with breadcrumbs, and then flavored by adding the dried fruit which gave it its name: dried plums (in other words, prunes), raisins, currants, sugar, ginger, other spices, and even wine. It was also served at the beginning of the Christmas meal, rather than the end.

During the eighteenth century this porridge became thicker and was boiled in a cloth. By the nineteenth century the meat component had gone completely and the dish was served as a dessert, doused in flaming brandy with a sprig of holly in the top.

It was during the Victorians' reinvention of Christmas that plum pudding found its place as a highlight of the Christmas meal. That renowned writer and re-inventor of Christmas, Charles Dickens, wrote about its importance and grandeur in *A Christmas Carol*:

> . . . like a speckled cannon-ball, so hard and firm, blazing in half a quarter of ignited brandy, and bedecked with Christmas holly stuck into the top. Oh, a wonderful pudding! Bob Cratchit said, and calmly too, that he regarded it as the greatest success achieved by Mrs. Cratchit since their wedding.

When Queen Victoria was on the throne, the British traveled to all corners of the globe, taking their traditions and customs with them. So the Christmas pudding traveled around the world too, becoming an intrinsic part of Christmas meals enjoyed by ex-pats living in Australia and British troops fighting in the Crimea. Even the poorhouses provided some manner of plum pudding for those incarcerated within on Christmas Day.

The traditional time to prepare the pudding to be eaten on Christmas Day was the last Sunday before Advent, called Stir-up Sunday. Each member of the family was supposed to take a turn at stirring the mixture, and make a wish while doing so.

But why was it called Stir-up Sunday? That might sound like a silly question now, but the name has nothing to do with people stirring Christmas pudding mixture. It actually comes from a passage in the Prayer Book related to Saint Andrew's Day: "Stir up, we beseech Thee, O Lord, the will of thy faithful people." Stir-up Sunday is usually also the one closest to Saint Andrew's Day, November 30, and perhaps it is because of this instruction from the Prayer Book that people have for so many years made their Christmas puddings on that particular day.

Of course brandy butter is as traditional as the Christmas pudding it usually accompanies, and if you fancy making it yourself this year, you can't go wrong with this simple recipe.

Brandy Butter

100 g/4 oz. butter
50 g/2 oz. icing sugar
1 tbs brandy

Cream the sugar and butter together, stir in the brandy, and then beat into the mix. Refrigerate until it's needed. And that's it!

WHO WERE THE THREE KINGS?

In the traditional Christmas story, acted out in Nativity plays year in year out around the country, the infant Jesus is visited by three kings who present him with expensive gifts full of symbolic meaning. But who actually were this trio of monarchs?

Well, this is something of an academic question really, as, according to scholars of the Bible, they weren't kings and there weren't three of them. For starters, of the four gospels in the Bible—those written by Matthew, Mark, Luke, and John—only two mention anything about Christ's birth. And then, just to complicate matters, Matthew and Luke—who did write about the Nativity—provide us with different parts of what has become the traditional Christmas story. Luke tells us about the shepherds and hosts of angels, while Matthew relates the part where the wise men come to worship the Christ child, and the holy family's resulting escape from the paranoid King Herod.

It is also interesting to note that the story of Jesus' birth was not as important to early Christians as his teachings and the events surrounding his death. Of the twenty-seven books in the New Testament, only two mention anything about the Nativity, and then only briefly. However, for many in our secular modern world, Christmas is the only Christian festival that is uniformly celebrated on any kind of scale.

But back to the kings . . . this is what Matthew has to say about the wise men's visit:

> After Jesus was born in Bethlehem in Judea, during the time of King Herod, wise men from the East came to Jerusalem and asked, "Where is the one who has been born king of the Jews? We saw his star in the east and have come to worship him" (Matthew 2:1–2).

At this point, the Bible seems clear that the baby Jesus' visitors were wise men. However, in some sources, these visitors are described as Magi, astrologers-cum-astronomers-cum-religious sages, so, in other words, priests. In fact, those who are knowledgeable about such matters agree that the Magi were Zoroastrian astrologer-priests, not kings. And there weren't three of them either.

Scholars still debate whether there were in fact only two wise men. (As they are mentioned in the plural we know there have to be at least two.) Others argue it was more like twenty, while Eastern tradition claims there were twelve. The familiar figure of three wasn't settled on by the Church until the sixth century.

It would appear that the confusion over the number of wise men came about because what the Bible *does* mention is that these far-ranging holy men brought the infant Christ three gifts. Early interpreters of the Bible, perhaps understandably, took this to mean that each gift had been given by one individual; hence three wise men.

This confusion may have been strengthened by the fact that in Psalm 72, kings from three different places—Tarshish, Sheba, and Seba—brought tribute to King Solomon and knelt before him (probably swearing fealty, as Solomon was effectively the super-power of his time in that part of the world).

And there is a third Biblical source which has helped create the traditional image of the three kings: that of the Book of Isaiah. It is Isaiah who prophesies Jesus' birth. Isaiah Chapter 60 also mentions gold and frankincense, two of the three gifts which Matthew says the wise men brought to Jesus, the last being myrrh.

And the prophet also mentions both kings and camels, although Matthew does not. So you can see how these references became jumbled together to create the image of the three kings that is a mainstay of Nativity plays to this day.

Thanks to the popular Christmas carol "We Three Kings" (actually properly titled "Kings of Orient"), most people are familiar with the fact that the three kings' names were Melchior, Caspar, and Balthazar. But if there weren't actually three kings, how did these names become associated with them?

Did you know . . .?

The merchant-explorer Marco Polo supposedly saw the graves of the three wise men during his incredible journey to China. The ornate tombs lay in the town of Saveh (now Tehran, in Iran). These shrines supposedly contained the preserved bodies of Melchior, Caspar, and Balthazar.

According to Polo's account, the kings each visited the infant Jesus separately. To each of them, Jesus appeared to be their age and size and it was only when they went back together that the Magi saw him as he really was, a baby.

The first literary source that mentions the names of the three kings is a chronicle dating from the sixth century called the *Excerpta Latina Barbari*. In it, the chronicler mentions the birth of Jesus and later goes on to say that "the Magi brought him gifts and venerated him. The Magi are called Bithisarea, Melchior, and Gaspar."

The more common spelling of Bithisarea was Balthazar, and Balthazar was a corruption of Belteshazzar—which was the name by which the prophet Daniel (as in the lions' den) was known at the Babylonian court. It is likely that the name Melchior is formed from the Hebrew words *melek* (meaning "king") and *or* (meaning "light"), making him the King of Light. As such he was the king who brought the baby Jesus a gift of gold, after the precious metal's dazzling brightness. Caspar, or Gaspar, may be a corruption of Godaphar. A character who appears in an apocryphal text known as the *Act of Thomas*, Godaphar was a famous Indian king.

It was a later written reference, which is found in the *Collectanea* (a book probably from Ireland and probably dating from the eighth century), which finally crystallized the now familiar image of three dignitaries from foreign lands. It has Melchior, the bringer of gold, as an old man with a white beard. Caspar, the bringer of frankincense, in contrast is seen as young and beardless, while Balthasar, the bringer of myrrh, is African and has a black beard.

In 2004, the General Synod of the Church of England consented to a revision of the Book of Common Prayer. A committee agreed that the term "Magi," as used in the Bible, was the name used for officials at the Persian court. This means that not only were Jesus' visiting Magi not kings, they did not number three, were possibly not even wise, and they might have been female as well!

WHERE DOES THE CHRISTMAS WREATH COME FROM?

To the pagan peoples of Europe, evergreens possessed magical powers; how else was it that the holly, fir, and ivy stayed green and kept their leaves in the depths of winter when other plants vanished and trees were left as leafless skeletons compared to the green glory of summer?

Some of these seemingly magical plants even produced fruit and flowers throughout the winter months. What other possible explanation could there be? So, understandably, in the freezing depths of winter when all other life seemed to have disappeared from the world, these same pagan peoples brought evergreens into their homes, partly to pay homage to their gods—who kept life going throughout these dark days—and partly in the hope that some of their magical protection might rub off on them.

Our Roman ancestors also considered evergreens lucky, and during the feast of Saturnalia (which took place around what is now Christmastime) they too decorated their homes with boughs of holly and the like. They were also fans of the laurel, which was supposed to have the power to protect and purify. Of course it also stood as a symbol of victory and honor and was used to decorate those who had achieved some form of distinction in Ancient Rome. (It is from this that we get the expression "resting on your laurels.")

Thanks to their connections with the concept of eternal life, it is easy to see how evergreens came to be such a central part of the

Christian feast of Christmas. After all, the Church teaches that Jesus rose from the dead to eternal life himself, and offers the same to his faithful servants.

There were also other, more immediate benefits to bringing evergreens inside. Pine branches gave the home a fresh, clean smell, and pine-scented air fresheners and sprays are still a popular choice today—particularly for the bathroom. Rosemary, the herb of remembrance (as mentioned by Ophelia in a scene from Shakespeare's *Hamlet*), added its own fragrant aroma. It was particularly appropriate as Christmas is also that time of year when people remember friends and family, as well as the birth of Jesus.

The presence of evergreen plants in the home during the festive season has lived on in several forms: through the Christmas tree, in carols such as "The Holly and the Ivy" and "Deck the Halls," and of course with the Christmas wreath.

Other evergreen rings were also transformed into symbols of the Christian Church. Branches of evergreens were twisted around a hoop which was then hung up. Candles were attached to the outer edge of the ring. When lit, and with the ring having been spun, the candle flames created a whirling circle of light. Pagan peoples believed that this magical symbol would banish the winter darkness, helping to hasten the lengthening days and new life that came with the spring. This evergreen ring subsequently became the Advent ring that appears in churches four Sundays before Christmas. One candle is lit each Sunday, with a fifth candle at the center of the ring being lit on Christmas Day.

How to make a Christmas wreath

1. First of all, make yourself a circular metal frame. This could be something as simple as a coat hanger bent out of shape.

2. Using wire or garden twine (or just plain old string) to hold it in place, cover the ring with sphagnum moss, (which you can acquire from a florist's).

3. Add green foliage to the ring, using plants like holly, ivy, and swathes of an evergreen, like fir.

4. Push stems of berries through the moss to add some color.

5. If you want, you can even add some seasonal flowers, such as Christmas roses.

6. Tie a loop of string to the back of the wreath or attach another piece of wire, so that you can hang it from your front door.

And there you have it: one Christmas wreath.

Did you know . . ?

The vibrantly colored Poinsettia, with its bright red leaves, that has become such a Christmas institution is named after the first American ambassador to Mexico, Dr. Joel Roberts Poinsett. In Mexico the plant goes by the name of the Flower of the Holy Night, but when Poinsett brought it back to America it was renamed in his honor.

In Mexico, the plant has legendary origins that are associated with Christmas. It was once the tradition in that country to place gifts for Jesus on church altars on Christmas Eve. One poor boy had nothing to give and, in his distress, knelt outside the church window and prayed. And there, where he had been kneeling, a beautiful plant with red leaves sprang up.

The town of Encinitas in California is known as the Poinsettia capital of the world because of the profusion of plants found there.

WHY ARE REINDEER SO
ASSOCIATED WITH
CHRISTMAS?

It may surprise you to learn that reindeer did not enter the Father Christmas story until the nineteenth century, and it was all the fault of the American Episcopalian minister Clement Clarke Moore. It was Moore who composed the famous poem "An Account of a Visit from Saint Nicholas" (a.k.a. "'Twas the Night Before Christmas"), as a Christmas treat for his own children. In his poem, Moore had a diminutive elf-like Santa pulled in a miniature sleigh by equally tiny reindeer.

At one point Santa reels off their now so familiar names, but which were new to those reading the poem when it first appeared in print back in 1823.

More rapid than eagles his coursers they came, and he whistled, and shouted, and called them by name:

"Now, Dasher! now, Dancer! now, Prancer and Vixen!
On, Comet! on Cupid! on, Donner and Blitzen!"

Moore was embarrassed by his poem, which is wholly secular and mentions nothing of the religious festival that inspired it, beyond the name of Saint Nicholas. At first he didn't take credit for it. However, by the 1830s it had really taken off. With children all over America expectantly awaiting a visit from Santa Claus on Christmas Eve as a result of his poem, Moore eventually decided it was time to come clean. In 1837 he claimed authorship when it was published in a book of poems, and it appeared in an anthology of his own work in 1844.

What is immediately apparent from a reading of "An Account of a Visit from Saint Nicholas" is the complete lack of an appearance by the red-nosed reindeer himself, Rudolph. That's because he wasn't an invention of Moore but appeared more than 100 years later.

"Rudolph the Red-Nosed Reindeer" first graced the page in 1939. It was a rather whimsical narrative poem, written with the express intention of drawing more customers into Montgomery Ward stores, and was the creation of Robert L. May, an American copywriter working for the department store chain. The eponymous reindeer subsequently appeared in an advertisement for the Chicago store.

Many people know of "Rudolph the Red-Nosed Reindeer" in the form of a song, but it wasn't set to music until

1949. The composer was called Johnny Marks and his musical version was recorded by "the singing cowboy" Gene Autry—a big deal at the time. The song has been recorded by hundreds of other artists since then and has sold more than 80 million records worldwide!

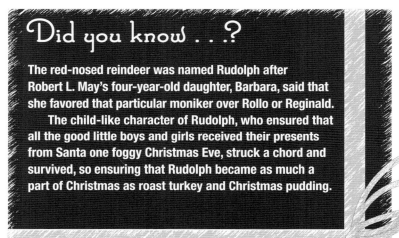

Did you know . . .?

The red-nosed reindeer was named Rudolph after Robert L. May's four-year-old daughter, Barbara, said that she favored that particular moniker over Rollo or Reginald.

The child-like character of Rudolph, who ensured that all the good little boys and girls received their presents from Santa one foggy Christmas Eve, struck a chord and survived, so ensuring that Rudolph became as much a part of Christmas as roast turkey and Christmas pudding.

Did you know . . .?

When "Rudolph the Red-Nosed Reindeer" was first published in 1939 it sold more than 2 million copies. When it was printed again after the end of the Second World War, in 1946, it sold another 3.5 million!

Ten things you probably didn't know about Rudolph and his friends

1. The reindeer is the only deer that can be domesticated, and was the first hoofed animal to be so. It provides the nomadic tribes who live within the Arctic Circle (such

as the Lapps) with milk, cheese, meat, fat, clothing, footwear, tools (made from the antlers and bones), highly durable bindings (made from the animal's sinews), and a means of transport.

2. The Finns once measured distance in terms of how far a reindeer could run without having to stop to urinate. The *poronkusema* is a measurement somewhere between 4 and 7 miles. The word *poronkusema* itself means "reindeer peeing."

3. A reindeer calf can outrun a man at only one day old.

4. Lady reindeer are the only females of any species of deer that have horns.

5. In Iceland, reindeer meat (or *hreindýr*) is becoming an increasingly popular Christmas dinner choice.

6. The Lapp people of Scandinavia believe that taking powdered reindeer antlers increases virility.

7. Reindeer are able to walk over snow without sinking into it because their weight is distributed over a large area thanks to their wide-splayed hooves.

8. One reindeer can pull twice its body weight up to 40 miles.

9. Reindeer are vegetarians by choice but when the supply of greenery runs out they will eat anything and everything, from eggs and shed antlers to placenta and even rodents!

10. And lastly, male reindeer lose their antlers in the winter; only the females and castrated males keep them. So either way, it's not looking good for Rudolph! Having a red nose was actually the least of his problems.

WHAT ARE THE TWELVE DAYS OF CHRISTMAS?

It is one of the most popular Christmas carols, telling of a zealous suitor's extravagant Christmas gifts to his sweetheart. But when do the actual twelve days of Christmas fall, and what is the true meaning of the carol's bizarre shopping list?

Let's start with the twelve days of Christmas themselves. Many people have come to believe that the twelve days of Christmas are those leading up to the main event on December 25. However, they are actually the days that come after it, with the last day being Epiphany (the date on which the Christian Church celebrates the visit of the Magi to the Christ child), which falls on January 6. This is why that date is also known as Twelfth Night.

This period of time has come to be known as both Twelve-tide and Christmastide. In Medieval England, it was a time of continuous feasting and merrymaking. There was always plenty of food to go around; at least there was plenty of meat to go around, as most animals were slaughtered come the winter to save the farmers the cost of having to feed them during the long winter months.

But what of the carol? There is a widely perpetuated myth that "The Twelve Days of Christmas" was one of the so-called catechism songs. The theory goes that during the period 1558–1829—when it was illegal to worship as a Catholic, with laws in place  preventing people from either publicly or privately practicing the faith of the Roman Church—certain songs were written with the express intention of teaching young Catholics the basic tenets of their faith, and some people believe that "The Twelve Days of Christmas" is one of these.

These believers insist that each of the otherwise frankly ludicrous gifts is a coded message representing a significant element of the Catholic catechism. In this case, the partridge in the pear tree is Jesus on the cross, the two turtle doves are the Old and New Testaments, while the three French hens represent the gifts of the Spirit mentioned in the first book of Corinthians—faith, hope, and love. The four calling birds are in fact the evangelists—Matthew, Mark, Luke, and John—the writers of the Gospels, and the five gold rings become the Jewish Torah, the first five books of the Bible which contained the laws that Jewish people should live by.

It goes on: the six geese a-laying are the six days of creation, while the seven swans a-swimming are the seven gifts of the Holy Spirit—wisdom, understanding, counsel, fortitude, knowledge, piety, and fear of the Lord God. The eight maids a-milking stand in for the eight beatitudes mentioned by Jesus in the Sermon on the Mount. The nine ladies dancing are the nine fruits of the Spirit listed in the Book of Galatians—love, peace, patience, kindness, goodness, faithfulness, gentleness, and self-control—and the ten lords a-leaping are in fact the Ten Commandments. The eleven pipers piping are the eleven faithful apostles (so don't include the traitorous Judas), and the twelve drummers drumming are the twelve points of belief expressed in the Apostles' Creed.

Only they don't mean that, not any of them, at least according to others. The truth is that there isn't any substantive evidence to either support the Catholic-teaching claim or to disprove it. What we do know is that the carol was a part of Christmas traditions in Europe and Scandinavia from as early as the sixteenth century. The familiar words of "The Twelve Days of Christmas" were also published in London, around the year 1780, in a collection of children's rhymes called *Mirth without*

Mischief. It was included in this context as a memory game with accompanying forfeits for the forgetful.

It's not just the origin and purpose of the carol that are a cause of confusion; the words themselves are even up for debate. In certain versions of the carol, the gifts of the last four days appear in a different order. Instead of nine ladies dancing, ten lords a-leaping, eleven pipers piping, and twelve drummers drumming, you could have nine drummers drumming, ten pipers piping, eleven ladies, or even dames, a-dancing, and the twelve lords a-leaping. There is even one variation in which ten fiddlers fiddle, so doing the pipers out of a job. The four calling birds can also be a problem. In some versions they are mockingbirds, while in others they are blackbirds. There is even some debate over the stalwart partridge, or at least its pear tree. The French for partridge is *perdrix* (pronounced *per-dree*) which could actually have made the original opening line, "A partridge, une perdrix."

Whatever the origins of the carol, "The Twelve Days of Christmas" is the source of much amusement in that it provides the basis for a suitably festive mathematical brainteaser, that of "How many gifts does the young lady, who narrates the carol, receive?" The gifts sent by the eager suitor referred to as "my true love" are cumulative.

The lucky lady receiving them doesn't just receive a partridge in a pear tree on day one and then two turtle doves the next. Looking at the lyrics closely, it soon becomes apparent that on day two his sweetheart receives two turtle doves and *another* partridge.

On the third day of Christmas she gets the French hens, another pair of turtle doves and yet another partridge, pear tree, the works. And so it goes on . . . Rather than receiving a total of 78 gifts over the twelve days, the narrator of the carol actually receives 364 individual items, one for each day of a traditional year, minus Christmas Day.

Did you know . . .?

There is a mathematical formula you can use to work out the total number of gifts given by the extravagant "my true love" celebrated in "The Twelve Days of Christmas" on any one day of the twelve days. Where N is a particular day out of the twelve, the total number of gifts given on that day = N(N+1)(N+2)/6.

People have had some fun with this over the years. Since 1984, PNC Wealth Management based in the United States has maintained the Christmas Price Index. This is a pricing chart that plots the current cost of one set of each of the gifts given by the "true love" of the carol. This has even been used as a more general economic indicator. However, it is also used to calculate the True Cost of Christmas, in other words the total cumulative cost of all the gifts listed, including repetitions. (The people mentioned in the song are hired, not purchased.) According to PNC, in 1984 the True Cost of Christmas for the romantically inclined was $61,318.94. However, by 2007 it had risen to $78,100.10.

There is a growing trend for people to buy more and more of their Christmas gifts online to save money. However, if the "true love" of the carol had done that in 2007 he would have actually been even worse off. The True Cost of Christmas purchased over the Internet would have set him back $128,886.00!

Did you know . . .?

The Mesopotamian holiday of Zagmuk lasted for twelve days and featured the symbolic sacrifice of the king (replaced by a convenient convict) which compensated for the sins of the people. Sound familiar?

WHY IS FISH EATEN ON CHRISTMAS EVE?

In many households it is still traditional to eat fish on Christmas Eve; but why? This custom is one of those that arose during a more religious time in our country's history. During the Middle Ages, it was the tradition to eat fish on a Friday (because Friday was a day of abstinence when the Catholic Church prohibited the consumption of meat) and this is still a not uncommon practice today.

For Catholics—the night of December 24 is the Vigil of the Nativity and, as such, is a fast. That being the case, meat is not to be eaten at this time either. However, our Medieval forebears did not consider fish to be meat, and so a fish dish is permissible.

During the reign of King Henry V (he of Agincourt and Sir Laurence Olivier fame), at one Christmas at court, a huge range of fish was consumed, everything from salmon, lobster, and roach to carp, lampreys, and pike!

Special kinds of fish are enjoyed throughout Europe on Christmas Eve. In Brittany, in France, cod is the fish of choice. In many parts of Germany and Styria it is carp, while herring salad is the favored dish in Saxony and Thuringia. Further afield, in Italy, a great supper—called the *cenone*—has fish at its center, with stewed eels being particularly popular.

But that was as nothing compared to what was eaten from Christmas Day to the feast of Saint John the Evangelist on December 27. During those three days, those spending Christmas at Prestbury managed to put away one boar, two and three-quarter cows, two calves, four doves, four pigs, sixty chickens and capons, eight partridges and two geese, and still found room for bread and cheese. Forty gallons of red wine were consumed, along with four gallons of white wine. How much ale (which was everyone's everyday beverage) was drunk is not recorded!

Of course Christmas Eve is probably best known as the night when Santa Claus delivers presents to those children who have been good during the previous year. However, there are many more traditions and customs associated with Christmas Eve above and beyond the visit of poor, over-burdened Santa Claus and his beleaguered team of reindeer.

A custom associated with Christmas Eve was that of the Dumb Cake. This was a very dumb cake indeed, as it was actually a kind of loaf that was baked on Christmas Eve by any single girl who wanted to find out who she was eventually going to marry.

For the magic of the Dumb Cake to work, the desperately seeking singleton had to make the cake alone and in silence. Once done, she pricked it with her initials and then went to bed, but leaving the door open. At the stroke of midnight, her husband-to-be was supposed to enter the house and prick his initials next to hers. A variation on this tradition had the young lady's intended entering the house and turning the cake as it cooked in the oven.

Christmas Eve has also long been the traditional time to deco-rate the house and put up the tree ready for Christmas morning. However, in our modern age it is a well-documented fact that Christmas starts earlier and earlier each year, so that trees and decorations festoon streets and department stores from as early as the beginning of October.

For many people, Christmas celebrations themselves start on Christmas Eve. For some nationalities, such as the people of Poland, it is the time when families gather to exchange gifts. For others, Christmas starts with Midnight Mass on Christmas Eve. At this time, bells are sometimes tolled to announce the death of the Devil and the coming of Christ.

Did you know . . .?

The Devil's Knell of Dewsbury in Yorkshire is a very special tolling. Each Christmas Eve the tenor bell of All Saints parish church, known as "Black Tom," is tolled once for every year since Christ's birth in the minutes leading up to Christmas. At midnight all the bells ring out in joyful celebration of the Devil's death!

Midnight is usually known as the witching hour, when fell powers hold sway over the land, but this rule is turned on its head on Christmas Eve. Evil spirits lose their powers and one Irish legend has it that at that time the gates of Heaven open so that anyone who dies at that selfsame hour will go straight to heaven, rather than having to wait until the last trump of Doomsday.

Did you know . . .?

In 1867, Macy's department store in New York City remained open until midnight on Christmas Eve for the first time, effectively initiating the tradition of last-minute Christmas shopping.

WHEN, AND WHY, WAS
CHRISTMAS CANCELED?

There is a classic, melodramatic line in the movie *Robin Hood, Prince of Thieves* when an enraged Sheriff of Nottingham (played by Alan Rickman, hamming it up to within an inch of his life) declares, in a moment of moustache-twirling villainy, "Cancel the kitchen scraps for lepers and orphans, no more merciful beheadings, and call off Christmas!"

What many people don't know is that Christmas *was* canceled, for real, but it wasn't in the twelfth or thirteenth century. It was in fact in the seventeenth century.

During the 1640s and '50s it was against the law to celebrate Christmas, with various pieces of legislation put in place making it illegal for churches to open on Christmas Day (unless it was a Sunday of course), for mince pies to be eaten and for people to decorate their houses with holly, ivy, and mistletoe. Many people have blamed the Lord Protector of England at this time, the king-killer Oliver Cromwell, for this cessation of festive fun, but in reality it was just part of the seventeenth century Puritan crackdown on fun and frivolity in general.

From the late sixteenth century onwards, many pious people had come to frown upon the pagan-themed Christmas celebrations; they disliked the extravagance, waste, disorder, sin, and immorality to which it inevitably led, and they saw it as a link back to Roman Catholicism—it was called Christ's Mass after all (mass being a specifically Catholic ceremony). The Puritans argued that there was nothing in the Bible that said God wanted the faithful to mark Christ's birth in any special way. And it wasn't only Christmas they wanted to get rid of because they thought it was ungodly. They had it in for Easter and Pentecost as well.

In the early 1640s, the Long Parliament had already begun to clamp down on Christmas, even changing its name to "Christ-tide," so as to distance themselves from the feast day's Catholic connections. Parliament said that if Christ-tide was to be kept at all, it should be as a day of fasting and prayer. It was business as usual when the Long Parliament convened on December 25, 1643. In 1644, parliament stressed that December 25 was to be kept as a time of fasting and humiliation, when the faithful should think on the sins of those who had turned the day into a feast in the past. Both Houses of Parliament attended intense fast sermons on December 25, 1644. That year Cromwell's administration passed an Act of Parliament that banned any form of celebration during the twelve days of Christmas.

However, strict Puritans took the greatest exception to the pagan elements making up the Christmas festivities, which, let's face it, was most of them. Christmas Day itself was dubbed "Satan's working day" by the more extreme members of the Puritan cause, or even the "Antichrist's Mass." They particularly loathed the idea of wassailing—the practice of going door-to-door carol-singing—which more often than not ended up as an out-of-control drunken revel.

In January 1645, parliament in England produced a new Directory of Public Worship which made it clear that Sundays were to be strictly observed as holy days, for the worship of God, and that there were to be no other "festival days, vulgarly called Holy Days." Accompanying legislation made it illegal for any other forms of worship or church services to take place, especially Christmas. In June 1647, the Long Parliament passed an Ordinance making it absolutely clear that the feasts of Christmas, Easter, and Pentecost were abolished.

During the 1650s further laws were passed. Christmas carols were banned, shops and markets were ordered to stay open on December 25, and those found holding or attending a special Christmas church service could be fined or put in the stocks—whether they were men, women, or children. In London, soldiers were ordered to patrol the streets and take any food suspected of being cooked for an illicit Christmas celebration, by force if necessary. Nativity scenes were banned as the worship of idols, and the use of the word "Christmas" itself was seen as taking the Lord's name in vain.

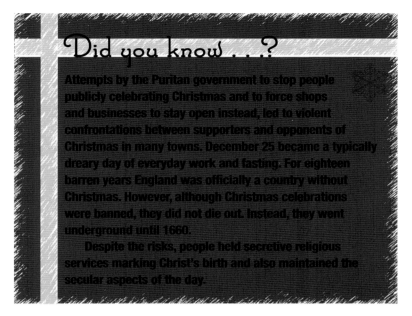

Did you know . . .?

Attempts by the Puritan government to stop people publicly celebrating Christmas and to force shops and businesses to stay open instead, led to violent confrontations between supporters and opponents of Christmas in many towns. December 25 became a typically dreary day of everyday work and fasting. For eighteen barren years England was officially a country without Christmas. However, although Christmas celebrations were banned, they did not die out. Instead, they went underground until 1660.

Despite the risks, people held secretive religious services marking Christ's birth and also maintained the secular aspects of the day.

With the Restoration of the monarchy in 1660, when Charles II took the throne of England, the Directory of Public Worship and all other anti-Christmas legislation brought in from 1642 to 1660 was declared null and void, and done away with. There are some historians who believe that the common man's desire to see the traditional, raucous Christmas celebrations restored helped lead to the Restoration of the monarchy! However, after eighteen years without a publicly recognized Christmas, the nation did not immediately resume the traditional feasting and other celebrations.

Enter William Winstanley, an Essex farmer's son, diarist and writer, and the man who saved Christmas. Under the pen-name of Poor Robin Goodfellow, Winstanley extolled the joys of Christmas. He believed that Christmas was a time for helping those worse off than oneself and, if it was celebrated properly, that it gave the poor and the destitute something to look forward to as the cold, dark days of winter drew on.

Winstanley was also a proponent of the traditional twelve days of Christmas, which began with the gathering of holly on Christmas Eve with which to decorate the home. A noted poet as well, he composed a rhyme for Christmas revelers to sing as they trooped home through the snow with the gathered greenery.

Now Christmas is come
Let us beat up the drum,

And call all our neighbors together.
And when they appear,
Let us make them such cheer
As will keep out the wind and the weather.

Everyone attended church on Christmas morning, to celebrate the Nativity, before returning home for the first of many feasts. Between Christmas Day and Twelfth Night, football matches took place against other villages, there was skating on frozen ponds, country walks, horse rides, and visits to other houses so that they might enjoy yet more festive hospitality.

Twelfth Night itself saw the return of wassailing, with songs being sung around the tallest tree in the apple orchard, which then had its roots drenched with cider for good luck. The twelve days of celebrating ended with a final supper of roast swan, followed by "caudle Sack posset"—a thick and very alcoholic custard.

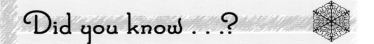

Did you know . . .?

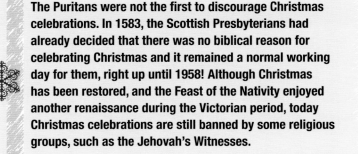

The Puritans were not the first to discourage Christmas celebrations. In 1583, the Scottish Presbyterians had already decided that there was no biblical reason for celebrating Christmas and it remained a normal working day for them, right up until 1958! Although Christmas has been restored, and the Feast of the Nativity enjoyed another renaissance during the Victorian period, today Christmas celebrations are still banned by some religious groups, such as the Jehovah's Witnesses.

Did you know . . ?

According to the Holy Days and Fasting Days Act of 1551, which has not yet been repealed, you cannot drive to mass on Christmas Day. You have to walk to church instead.

You also shouldn't take part in any sports, except for archery. Henry VIII banned all forms of sport on Christmas Day, other than archery, but then bluff King Hal himself didn't practice what he preached, as he was rather partial to a game of footie!

And under a law enacted by Elizabeth I in 1588 you should only have goose for Christmas dinner; she made it an offense to eat any other bird on Christmas Day.

WHAT IS A YULE LOG?

The Yule log, either in the form of a small wood and holly sprig centerpiece placed on the table during Christmas dinner or in its guise as a chocolate dessert, is still a popular part of Christmas, particularly among those with a sweet tooth.

To our pagan ancestors living in the frozen north of Europe and Scandinavia, the dark days of winter were a frightening time. The night was the domain of demons and malicious spirits. On top of that, Odin, chief among the Norse gods, flew through the sky on his eight-legged horse Sleipnir, looking down at the world with his furious one-eyed gaze, deciding who should prosper and who should perish in the year ahead.

The sensible choice was to stay inside at this time of year, safe from the horrors that lurked outside. To help keep the darkness at bay, on or around December 21, the time of the winter solstice, fathers and sons would go out into the forests and bring back the largest log they could find. This massive piece of timber was then put on the fire and left to burn for the entirety of the season of Yule —twelve days altogether.

Yule was the name given to the Viking winter feast, a time when light and new birth were celebrated in the face of the darkness and death witnessed in the natural world. It was at this time that evergreens were brought into the house; a sign that life persisted, even during these dying days of the year.

However, despite the deeply felt need to keep unwanted spirits outside, in Scandinavia people also believed that the burning Yule log warmed the frozen shades of the family's dearly departed,

who returned to the ancestral home every Christmas Eve. Some families even went to the trouble of laying a place for them at the dinner table.

In England, the preferred wood for the Yule log was ash, while in Scotland birch was favored. As well as keeping everyone warm and providing heat to cook by, the Yule log was also a symbol of prosperity to come; every spark that fell from it was supposed to represent a pig or calf to be born in the spring.

In Germany, the Yule log miraculously had the power to protect a home from lightning, and whenever a storm threatened, the stump of the *Christbrand* (as it was called after Germany's conversion to Christianity) was rekindled.

As long as the Yule log burned, feasting and revelry were in order. But should the log go out, then bad fortune would fall upon the household, for it was then that Old Night and its minions would sneak inside to do their mischief.

The English word "Yule" is a corruption of the Old Norse *Jo⁻l*. However, *Jo⁻l* itself may derive from *hjól*, meaning "wheel." In this sense, it refers to the moment when the wheel of the year is at its lowest point, in midwinter, ready to rise again in the spring.

Despite the Christianizing of the winter solstice, the Yule log remained an important feature of the festive season. The old gods might have gone, replaced by Christianity, but the ancient superstitious fears surrounding the dark had not!

To the Celtic mind, when the days were at their shortest, at the end of December, the sun itself stood still and it was only by keeping the Yule log burning for those twelve days that the sun would deign to return and the days grow longer once more. So it was that by the Middle Ages the log would be hauled into the house on Christmas Eve, with great pomp and ceremony, and lit using a piece of the previous year's log, saved for just this purpose.

By the nineteenth century in England the custom had changed, as so many did under the influence of the more practically minded Victorians. Now, rather than burning for twelve days, the Yule log only had to last twelve hours, and in some homes the log was replaced by a candle (candles having their own symbolic connections with the Star of Bethlehem).

Of course, now the Yule log has become the edible Christmas log. For any chocolate lover it has to be one of the highlights of the festive fare that gets wheeled out—better even than Christmas cake! And if you're one such admirer of the cocoa bean, then you should try this recipe yourself.

Chocolate Christmas Log

175 g/6 oz. butter
175 g/6 oz. plain chocolate
140 ml/¼ pint of double cream
100 g/3½ oz. caster sugar
75 g/3 oz. plain flour
75 g/3 oz. icing sugar
4 eggs
4 tbs rum
1 tbs cocoa powder
1 tbs vanilla essence
2 drops almond essence
Icing sugar

Start by greasing and lining a 13 × 9 in. Swiss roll tin and pre-heat the oven to 395°F. Cream the eggs and sugar together in a large bowl before folding in the sifted flour and cocoa powder. Transfer the whole lot to the tin and bake for 12 to 15 minutes, until the cake has risen and turned golden. Take it out and allow to cool, but only slightly.

Place a sheet of greaseproof paper on a dampened cloth and sprinkle caster sugar on it. Turn the cake out onto the sheet, trim the edges, and roll it up. Allow the cake to cool further. Then, whisk together the double cream, rum, and both the vanilla and almond essence until stiff. Gently unroll the cake again and spread it with the cream filling. Roll it up once more.

Cream together the butter, icing sugar, and chocolate, then cover the cake with the mixture. Sprinkle your finished chocolate log with icing sugar and chill in the fridge for one hour before serving. Garnish with a sprig of holly.

WHAT WAS THE FIRST NOËL?

The first Nowell the angel did say
　　Was to certain poor shepherds in fields as they lay;
In fields where they lay tending their sheep,
On a cold winter's night that was so deep.
Nowell, Nowell, Nowell, Nowell,
Born is the King of Israel.

We hear it sung of in carols every year, from the familiar "The First Nowell" to the obscure, such as "Sir Christèmas." But what does Noël mean? And what was the first one?

Delving into the origins of "The First Nowell" raises almost as many questions as it answers. Certainly there is much doubt over the carol's origins, as well as the uncertainty regarding the meaning and origin of the word "Nowell."

Some believe that the English word "Nowell" comes from the French *Noël* meaning "Christmas," which is itself from the Latin *natalis*, meaning "birth." However, others think that *Noël* is actually the French version of the English Nowell, which they believe comes from the Anglo-Saxon, and means "now all is well."

Then again, it may also originate from two Gaulish words, *noio* or *neu* (both meaning "new") and *helle* (meaning "light"), and instead refers to the winter solstice, after which the days start to lengthen again, with sunlight banishing the darkness. Or perhaps it is a combination of all of these.

So, in the context of the carol, it would appear that the angel was telling the shepherds that all was now well because the Christ child had been born. But whatever its meaning, "The First Nowell" surely refers to the first-ever Christmas, when Jesus Christ was born (even though he probably wasn't born in the middle of winter at all), and the first Nowell itself was the first time that God announced to the faithful through his divine messenger that all was well. Take your pick.

It is harder to pinpoint the origins of the carol, however. It is generally considered to have been written in or around the sixteenth or seventeenth century, although it could date from as far back as the thirteenth century, and its actual author remains unknown. The song was at first handed down orally and didn't appear in print until the 1800s. The familiar form of the carol that everyone knows today actually originated in Cornwall, appearing in *Some Ancient Christmas Carols* ten years before *Gilbert and Sandys' Christmas Carols* (1833). This later collection was edited by William B. Sandys, while the carols were arranged and edited by Davies Gilbert, who also wrote extra lyrics for some of them. The melody is believed to be a corruption of an earlier tune that would have been sung in a church gallery during services.

The composer Ralph Vaughan Williams notably included "The First Nowell" in the concluding movement of his "Christmas masque" *On Christmas Night* (which was based upon Dickens' *A Christmas Carol*) and his Nativity play *The First Nowell.*

Of course, the true stars of the carol are the shepherds to whom the angel makes its special announcement in the first verse. These shepherds represent the common man and particularly the Gentiles (those people who are not Jewish), which is why they play such an important role in the Christmas story.

However, in the first printed version of the carol, the line actually states that there were "three poor shepherds." Legends surround the identity of these individuals, just as there are stories told regarding the identity of the three wise men.

In his own note on the text of the carol, William Sandys remarks:

> According to some legends, the number [of shepherds] was four, called Misael, Achael, Cyriacus, and Stephanus, and these, with the names of the three Kings, were used as a charm to cure the biting of serpents, and other venomous reptiles and beasts. Something to bear in mind next time you take a stroll through adder country.

WHAT HAVE HOLLY
AND IVY GOT TO DO
WITH CHRISTMAS?

Well, of course, for starters, there's the popular carol "The Holly and the Ivy" that's sung at Christmas:

The holly and the ivy
When they are both full grown;
Of all the trees that are in the wood
The holly bears the crown.
O the rising of the sun
And the running of the deer,
The playing of the merry organ,
Sweet singing in the choir.
The holly bears a blossom
As white as any flower;
And Mary bore sweet Jesus Christ
To be our sweet savior.
The holly bears a berry
As red as any blood;
And Mary bore sweet Jesus Christ
To do poor sinners good.
What is myrrh anyway?
The holly bears a prickle
As sharp as any thorn;
And Mary bore sweet Jesus Christ
On Christmas Day in the morn.
The holly bears a bark
As bitt'r as any gall;
And Mary bore sweet Jesus Christ
For to redeem us all.

Although this oh-so-familiar carol is called "The Holly and the Ivy," when you come to look at it, it is blatantly only about the holly. But that still doesn't explain why both holly and ivy have become so inextricably connected with Christmas.

The main reason is that they are both evergreens, like the fir tree and the boughs used to form the traditional Christmas wreath and, as such, their significance dates back to pagan times. The Romans believed that both holly and ivy brought good luck and so decorated their homes with the plants during the festival of Saturnalia. They would also give sprigs of the plants to friends and loved ones as good luck tokens.

In time, the Church took these traditional elements of the extant winter festivals and gave them a Christian twist, adding their own symbolism. The sharp leaves of the holly came to represent Christ's crown of thorns, while the red berries were drops of his blood. The nascent Church was so successful in modifying the symbolism of the holly that in Scandinavia it is still known as the "Christ-thorn."

Other legends were invented, linking Christ to the holly. One stated that there had been a holly tree growing outside the stable where the infant Jesus was born. The tree was bare of berries, hungry birds having eaten them all. However, as soon as Jesus was born the tree grew new buds again, then flowers, and finally berries—all in the space of that one night.

Another tale had it that the shepherds who visited the infant Christ left behind a lamb as a gift, corralling it within a pen of holly branches. The lamb had other ideas, however, and forced its way out of the enclosure to return to the hill pastures with its mother. In doing so, the poor thing tore its coat, the sharp prickles of the holly drawing blood from the creature. It being a cold night, the drops of blood froze, becoming the holly's red berries.

To the Medieval mind, the holly and the ivy had other important characteristics. The holly represented the male—with its tough, woody stems and sharp prickles—while the ivy was supposed to be female—clinging and feeble. People believed that whichever plant was brought into the house first on Christmas Eve (as it was unlucky to bring either into your home *before* then) would be in charge for the following year. If the holly was brought in first, the man would be the boss, but if the ivy entered before the holly, the woman would be head of the household.

Holly was the more important of the two plants. It was supposed to protect a home from lightning, and so was often planted outside the front door. And it had even more miraculous powers; its red berries were able to detect evil and so the holly could offer protection against witches. Medieval men also believed that it had powers like those purported to be possessed by certain deodorant sprays today; carrying the leaves or berries about his person supposedly made a young man irresistible to the ladies.

And of course, in the carol "The Holly and the Ivy," the point is made none-too-subtly that the plant that represents the male is the most important! However, there were a number of carols written in the fifteenth century that had a different emphasis, although the ivy still often came off the worst. Nay, Ivy, nay it shall not be, indeed, Let Holly have the mastery, as the manner is. Holly stand in the hall, fair to behold; Ivy stand without the door, she is bitterly cold:

Nay, luy, nay, hyt shal not
be, iwys;
Let holy hafe the maystry, as
the maner ys.
Holy stond in the hall, fayre
to behold;

Iuy stond without the dore;
she ys ful sore a-cold.

Holy and hys mery men,
they dawnsyn and they syng;
Iuy and hur maydenys, they
wepyn and they wryng.
Iuy hath a kybe, she kaght yt
with the colde;
So mot they all haf ae that
with Ivy hold.
Holy hat berys as rede as anyrose;
The foster, the hunters kepe
hem fro the doos.
Iuy hath berys as blake as any
slo;
Ther com the oule and ete hym
as she goo.
Holy hath byrdys, a ful fayre
flok,
The nyghtyngale, the
poppynguy, the gayntyl
lauyrok.
Gode Iuy, what byrdys ast
thou?
Non but the howlat, the kreye,
"How, how!"

Holly and his merry men, they dance and they sing;
Ivy and her maidens, they weep and they wring [their hands].
Ivy has a chilblain, she caught
it with the cold;
So may they all have always,
that with Ivy hold.

Holly has berries as red as any rose;
The forester, the hunters keep them from the does.
Ivy has berries as black as any sloe;
There came the owl and ate them as she goes.
Holly has birds, a full fair flock;
The nightingale, the green woodpecker, the gentle lark.
Good Ivy, what birds have you?
None but the owlet that cries
"Hoo, hoo."

Secular carols like this one would have been accompanied by dancing, with the men and women facing each other as they sang the parts of the holly and the ivy. As can be seen in the example, the lyrics emphasized the difference between the sexes.

Being the less popular of the two plants, ivy was normally left outside, used only to decorate the outside of the house, while boughs of holly decked the halls inside. Ivy being cast in the role of the female may date back to Roman times and the cult of Bacchus, the god of wine and drunkenness. Bacchus was attended by a fanatical band of women called the Bacchae who, after consuming a concoction made from the juice of crushed ivy leaves and toxic toadstools, would go on an intoxicated rampage, while the god himself wore a crown of ivy leaves. Ivy was also associated with death, due to the fact that it can cling to anything as it grows and is often seen covering tombstones in graveyards.

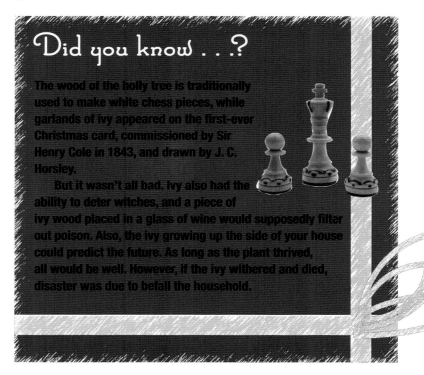

Did you know . . .?

The wood of the holly tree is traditionally used to make white chess pieces, while garlands of ivy appeared on the first-ever Christmas card, commissioned by Sir Henry Cole in 1843, and drawn by J. C. Horsley.

But it wasn't all bad. Ivy also had the ability to deter witches, and a piece of ivy wood placed in a glass of wine would supposedly filter out poison. Also, the ivy growing up the side of your house could predict the future. As long as the plant thrived, all would be well. However, if the ivy withered and died, disaster was due to befall the household.

WHAT IS MULLED WINE?

There's nothing quite like a little of your favorite tipple to warm your cockles, and when you've been out in the cold of a December night nothing warms the cockles quite like a glass of mulled wine.

Mulled wine has a long history, being lauded in Europe since at least the fifth century AD, and appearing in various forms in cook books from the sixteenth century onwards. To "mull" means "to heat and spice," although the origin of the word is uncertain. There is a Middle English word, *mollen*, which means "to moisten" or "crumble," but how this might connect with heating and spicing things up isn't clear.

It's not just wine that can be mulled, of course. Other traditional mulling recipes include those for mead, cider, and beer. Mulled wine and mulled beer used to be heated by plunging a red hot poker from the fire into it. It is worth remembering that the "mull" should never be allowed to get too hot and should most definitely never boil, otherwise the flavor will be spoiled and, worse than that, the alcohol will evaporate.

In Medieval times, people enjoyed a mulled drink called Ypocras, Hipocris, or Hippocras. It was named after the Greek physician Hippocrates, dubbed the "Father of Medicine," who was supposed to have devised the first recipe for it.

During the Middle Ages, Hippocrates had an almost mythical reputation for being able to heal—more magic and mysticism than medicine. As a consequence, Ypocras itself was generally accepted as being some kind of magical elixir for maintaining good health in general, with doctors recommending that it be enjoyed at the end of a meal as an aid to digestion.

Ypocras, and other drinks like it, were believed to be particularly good for keeping away all manner of ills throughout the cold winter months. There is probably some truth in this, for at the time it was certainly safer to drink the wine than the water. The practice of heating the drink would have helped to kill many of the unpleasant microbes merrily creating their own bit of culture within the wine. And wine did have a tendency to go bad: adding spices and honey would have made it palatable again.

The following is a modern take on the recipe for making this popular Medieval drink:

Ypocras

1 bottle of sweet red or white wine
1 to 2 cups of honey
1 tbs each of ginger, cinnamon, cardamom, white pepper, cloves, nutmeg, and caraway seeds
A cheesecloth

Bring the wine and honey close to a boil in a pan, skimming off the scum as it rises to the surface. Taste the concoction and add more honey to sweeten, if desired. Take off the heat and stir in the spices. Leave it to sit for 24 hours, while covered.

During this time the spices form a thick residue at the bottom of the pan. Now, using a ladle, decant the wine into a second container, straining it through 2 to 3 layers of cheesecloth, while trying to leave as much of the spice residue in the pan as possible. Store for 1 month before serving—the older it is, the better it tastes!

By the 1500s, recipes began to appear in cookbooks for mulling Clarrey (also spelt "clarree" or "claree"), another drink made using wine, honey, and spices. Both Clarrey and Ypocras are mentioned by the fourteenth-century poet Geoffrey Chaucer. From *The Merchant's Tale* we get the following rhyming couplet:

He drynketh ypocras, clarree, and vernage
Of spices hot, to increase his courage.

The name comes from the Latin *vinum claratum*, meaning "clarified wine," and it lives on today as "claret," which is a dry red wine. The original Clarrey, however, can be made with either red or white wine, as it is in this particular recipe.

Clarrey

1 bottle of inexpensive, sweet white wine
1 to 2 cups of honey
1 tbs each of cinnamon, galingale (or you could substitute ginger), and cardamom
1 tsp of white pepper
A cheesecloth

Bring the wine and honey close to a boil, then reduce the heat and skim off the scum as it rises. Taste and add honey for sweetness as required. Remove from the heat, stir in all of the spices, and then cover and allow to sit for 24 hours. As with the Ypocras, after this time you will need to use a ladle to transfer the liquid into another container, passing it through a strainer lined with 2 to 3 layers of cheesecloth to remove the spices. Again, leave behind as much as possible of the spice residue that will have formed in the bottom of the pot. Bottle it and store for 1 month before serving. A good Clarrey is one that has been aged for a year or even longer.

Bishop's punch—once called "bischopswyn"—is a traditional Christmas drink associated with Ol' Saint Nick. In countries where the feast day of Saint Nicholas is observed on December 6, such as in the Netherlands, revelers toast the original Father Christmas with it. If you fancy doing the same, try this recipe.

Bishop's Wine

1 bottle of red wine
1 cinnamon stick
Sugar to taste

1 orange stuck with cloves
The peel of 1 lemon

Place the clove-stuck orange in a large pan; add the red wine and leave to steep for half a day. During this time the wine will take on the flavors of the orange and cloves. Then you need to add the other ingredients together and simply warm the whole lot through half an hour before serving.

Popular in Sweden, Norway, Denmark, Finland, and Estonia, and drunk during Advent, *Glögg* is the Scandinavian form of mulled wine. Made from red wine, spices, and sugar, it can also have stronger spirits such as brandy, akvavit, or vodka added to it. It is served with raisins, almonds, and gingerbread biscuits.

Glögg can be made as a non-alcoholic drink, either by boiling it to evaporate the alcohol or by replacing the wine with black-currant juice. However, in the recipe presented here, the alcohol remains very much intact.

Glögg

1 bottle of red wine
25 g/1 oz. dried orange zest
25 g/1 oz. cinnamon sticks
20 cardamom seeds
12 cloves
200 g/8 oz. blanched almonds
200 g/8 oz. raisins
225 g/½ lb. brown sugar
70 ml/2½ fl. oz. brandy
A cheesecloth

Bring the wine close to a boil in a pot. Put the orange, cinnamon, cardamom, and cloves in the cheesecloth, tie it into a bundle and boil it in the pot for 15 minutes. Add the almonds and raisins, and cook for another 15 minutes, before removing the pan from the heat. Add the brown sugar and brandy, and stir them in. Then remove the spice bundle. Serve hot.

WHY ARE SPROUTS EATEN WITH CHRISTMAS DINNER?

Picture the scene. You sit down to dinner on Christmas Day, looking forward to tucking into turkey with all the trimmings; your plate is piled high with roast potatoes, parsnips, sausages wrapped in bacon, all smothered with gravy; and then the lurid green balls of bitterness move into view. Brussels sprouts.

Children hate them, as do most adults, and yet you have to have them as part of your otherwise utterly delicious Christmas dinner. And why? Because they're traditional! And besides, you've no doubt been told that they're good for you too.

Did you know . . .?

According to one survey carried out in 2002, brussels sprouts were the most hated vegetable in England. But whose fault is it that you have to sit through the most magnificent meal of the year dreading the fact that at some point you're going to have to pop one of those malodorous mini-cabbages into your mouth?

Brussels sprouts are unusual in that they are one of the few vegetables to have originated in northern Europe. They are members of the *Brassica* family (which also includes cabbages, cauliflowers, broccoli, and kale), cultivated first from the wild cabbage. They also just happen to come into season during the winter and are supposedly best harvested later on in the season, after they have suffered a few sharp frosts. In times gone by, the only fresh vegetables you could eat during the winter were those which were in season at that time of year, and sprouts fitted the bill at Christmastime.

But what has Brussels, capital of Belgium and the European Union, got to do with sprouts? Well, the first written reference to brussels sprouts comes from 1587. They became known as brussels sprouts because it is believed that they were widely cultivated in that part of Belgium in the sixteenth century.

When it comes to cooking them, it is common practice to cut them with a cross on their base. Most cooks who carry out this practice, before dropping the sprouts into boiling water, will tell you they do so to ensure that the inside will cook at the same rate as the outside. However, current culinary thinking has it that crossing the sprout in this way results in a loss of flavor. However, there is another reason why they are crossed, and that, like so many Christmas traditions, is based on good old-fashioned paranoid superstition.

It's supposed to keep the Devil out (but as far as this writer's concerned, the Devil's welcome to them). If you've ever wondered why sprouts are so blighted with "a powerful smell of drains," as the Victorians euphemistically put it, it's all down to chemistry.

During cooking, sprouts release sulphuric compounds which have that all-too-familiar and none-too-pleasant smell of rotten eggs. However, they can smell even worse *after* they've been eaten! These same chemical compounds react with bacteria in the gut to produce hydrogen sulphide, which is the constituent ingredient of stink bombs.

Other than that rather nasty aromatic side effect, it's no wonder that children don't like sprouts. Your sensitivity to tastes tends to decrease as you get older and, as a result, sprouts really are more distasteful to children than they are to adults. There's a perfectly acceptable scientific reason why the little green devils taste so bad: their bitter taste is a chemical defense evolved by the *Brassica oleracea* to stop insects from attacking it. So yes, sprouts *are* traditional—having arisen out of a traditional necessity to eat during the cold winter months—and what's more, they're good for you too.

Brussels sprouts, like cabbages, are members of the cruciferous family of vegetables, which are a good source of the antioxidant vitamins A and C, potassium and iron. They also contain something called sinigrin, which may, according to some sources, help to prevent bowel cancer. Good news for sprout farmers and those keen on keeping healthy, but bad news for anyone who doesn't like eating their greens, as to gain their full benefit you have to eat about 10 oz. (280 g) of sprouts a day.

Did you know . . . ?

In 2007, gastro-genius Heston Blumenthal created a Christmas meal like no other for six celebrity diners: actor Richard E. Grant, comedians Rob Brydon, Sue Perkins and Dara O'Briain, journalist Kirsty Wark, and broadcaster Terry Wogan. The meal went as follows:

- *Mulled wine* Hot on one side of the glass, cold on the other
- *Edible baubles* Made of blown sugar, filled with smoked salmon mousse
- *Gold, frankincense, and myrrh* Langoustine, onion, and vermouth stock cubes, wrapped in edible gold leaf and dissolved in frankincense water, served with a carved myrrh-wood spoon
- *Babe in a manger* Communion wafer sprayed with the aroma of freshly washed baby
  Flaming whiskey sorbet Scented with the perfume of a wood-paneled room, complete with roaring fire and leather armchair
- *Hand-reared roast goose* Goose fed on apple powder, Paxo stuffing, and essential oil of Christmas tree, accompanied by sherbet fountains made from the powdered goose feed with vanilla straws. Pommes purées with goose, chestnut, and bacon velouté. Served in a bell jar containing the smoky aroma of roasted chestnuts
- *Reindeer milk ice cream* Frozen in liquid nitrogen

WHY DO WE DISPLAY
NATIVITY SCENES AT
CHRISTMAS?

Nowadays, the sight of a Nativity scene with the baby Jesus, Mary, Joseph, and assorted livestock alongside visiting herdsmen and foreign dignitaries is indelibly etched onto the memory of anyone who has celebrated Christmas. Many homes dust off the figures of their own manger scene when they bring out the rest of their Christmas decorations. It can be seen in shopping centers and on the streets of towns across the country—not to mention on endless Christmas cards—and is an expected element of any church. There are even specific Nativity services held on or around Christmas Eve.

In one sense it is very obvious how such a tradition arose, when you consider the "facts" of the Christmas story told and re-told year after year. But in another way, it might seem a curious practice to keep up when so few people actually attend church on Christmas Day, as its religious significance continues to diminish in the modern age.

The first Nativity scene, created inside a church, was in Rome in the tenth century, at the Church of Santa Maria Maggiore. The idea soon caught on and other churches began creating their own stable scenes in time for the feast of Christ's Mass.

With the help of a local landowner, Gionvanni Velita, and his friends, Francis succeeded in creating his own representation of the Nativity in a cave, surrounded by candles. Details of the actual participants in his Nativity scene vary, with some saying that Francis used statues to represent the holy family, while others claim that real people, dressed in appropriate costumes, fulfilled the role. However, all the sources agree on the fact that at the centre of the scene was a straw-filled manger surrounded by real animals.

The people of Greccio came to the cave at nightfall on Christmas Eve, bearing candles and torches before them, to attend a Mass held there by Saint Francis. Saint Bonaventure, Francis' biographer, recounts how the experience was incredibly moving for those present, to the point where the people were

According to legend, the animals who were sharing the stable where Jesus was born, having seen the Holy Infant, suddenly found themselves able to speak. Every Christmas Eve since, farmyard animals the world over find their voices again and converse freely. However, human beings, who are such poor listeners anyway, shouldn't listen to them; it's considered bad manners, and to top it all, it brings bad luck. *Baaaa* humbug! However, one man is credited with creating the Christmas crib more than any other, and that is the thirteenth-century Saint Francis of Assisi. In 1220, Francis made the pilgrimage to Bethlehem. While there, he saw how Christmas was celebrated in the town of Jesus' birth and was so impressed that he asked the Pope, Honorius III, if he might recreate something like it in his own Italian home of Greccio.

"filled with the utmost joy, and shedding tears of devotion and compassion."

After Saint Francis' death, the custom of having a Christmas crib spread throughout Europe, with smaller wooden Nativity scenes popping up in churches and homes across the continent. By the seventeenth century, the custom of having a representation of the crib in the home was well-established and highly popular. In England it was even enhanced by the baking of crib pies—precursors of the modern mince pie—made in the shape of a cradle and sometimes with the addition of a little pastry baby Jesus.

Manger scenes almost always have the holy family of Mary, Joseph, and the infant Jesus in either a barn or a cave, with a donkey and ox present. On top of that there may also be a couple of shepherds in attendance, along with a lamb, and the three wise men. Some scenes even go to the lengths of adding a camel for the travelers from distant lands, a smattering of angels, and possibly even the Star of Bethlehem shining overhead.

However, in Catalonia, Spain, and the Basque Country, there is always another character present, without fail: the *caganer*. This grotesque individual, who is sometimes a caricature of an unpopular public figure, has nothing to do with the Nativity story but is merely a  reflection of the Catalans' irreverent sense of scatological humor. *Caganer* means "crapper," and the figure is that of a squatting man doing his business in the straw, hidden at the back of the stable.

WHAT IS WASSAILING?

Here we come a-wassailing
Among the leaves so green,
Here we come a-wandering,
So fair to be seen.
Love and joy come to you,
And to you your wassail too,
And God bless you, and send you
A happy New Year,
And God send you
A happy New Year.

Wassailing used to be a popular part of the Christmas festivities in England and the memory of it still lingers in the words of certain carols, but what was wassailing, and how exactly did people go about it?

Wassail itself was a hot drink which pre-dates the Christian festival by some centuries. The word "wassail" comes from the Old English *wæs hæl* which literally meant "be whole" and so, by extension, "be healthy." The phrase "hale and hearty" has its origins in this expression as well.

The ceremony from which wassailing developed was a toast to the sun as it rose on the morning after the shortest day of the winter solstice. It, like the veneration of evergreens, was believed to encourage a bountiful harvest (specifically that of fruit) in the year to come. The transformation of the winter festival to a Christian one did nothing to diminish the popularity of the wassail toast and it persisted, like so much else, becoming interwoven with the newer Christianized celebrations.

In Saxon, England, at the start of the year, the lord of the manor would shout the greeting *wæs hæl* to his assembled household, who would respond with the words *drinc hæl*, meaning "drink and be healthy." His lordship would then take a swig from a large wooden bowl—the wassail bowl or wassail cup—before passing it on to the next most senior member of the household. And so it would be passed down the line until everyone had had a drink.

Did you know . . .?

The expression "to drink a toast" actually has its origins in the wassail. By the time the practice of wassailing had left the lord's manor, with bands of peasants taking their empty wassail bowl from house to house for it to be filled with drink, the wassailers were sometimes given pieces of toast—rather like croutons—to float on the top. Each wassailer in turn took a piece and wished his fellows good cheer before eating the toast and washing it down with a swig of the potent mixture in the bowl. Hence the phrase "to drink a toast."

The fact that a drink whose constituent ingredient is ale should be called wassail is purely a coincidence. Apples are an important component of the recipe, along with spices and sugar, which was added late in the drink's development when it became more widely available.

Wassail

6 cups of ale
1 cup of sugar
Pinch of cinnamon
Pinch of ginger
Pinch of cloves
Pinch of nutmeg
6 beaten eggs
4 roasted apples

Heat the ale in a saucepan, add the sugar and spices, and bring almost to a boil. Take it off the heat and gradually add a little of the hot mixture to the beaten eggs. Return it to the saucepan and cook, this time stirring constantly until the mixture has thickened slightly. Put the roasted apples in a punch bowl (which must be heat-proof) and pour the mixture over them.

Due to its unusual mix of ingredients—which could include whipping cream instead of eggs—the contents of the wassail cup often had a frothy, foamy appearance. This gave the wassail drink its other name of "lamb's wool." Here is a variation on the wassail recipe which goes by that name.

Lamb's Wool

6 bottles of brown ale
1 cup of sherry
450 g/1lb. light brown sugar
2 roasted apples, sliced
1 lemon, sliced
½ tsp ginger
½ tsp cinnamon
½ a nutmeg
2 slices of toasted white bread

Heat one bottle of ale. Put the sugar in a large heat-proof bowl and stir well. Grate the half a nutmeg into the sugar-ale mixture, add cinnamon and ginger, then the sherry and the rest of the ale. Leave to stand for several hours. Before serving, finish it off with the sliced lemon and apples and float pieces of the toasted bread on top.

As an alternative to the traditional ale-based wassail or lamb's wool, you might want to try this West Country recipe for mulled cider.

Mulled Cider

1 liter/2 pints of still cider
2 small eating apples
4 cloves
140 ml/¼ pint of water
50 g/2 oz. soft brown sugar
1 cinnamon stick
1 tsp ground ginger
2 tangerines

Stick the apples with two of the cloves each and then bake. Heat the cider and, at the same time, heat the other ingredients (minus the orange) until all the sugar has dissolved, and then simmer for 5 minutes. Place the baked apples and tangerine pieces in a heat-proof punch bowl, strain the spiced water into it and lastly add the hot cider. If you have children among your household who would like to partake of the wassail, or you need to keep a clear head yourself (perhaps it's your turn to be the designated Christmas driver), then why not try the alcohol-free version overleaf.

By Tudor times, wassailing peasants had become a menace, with the drunken common folk weaving their way from the home of one rich landowner to another, singing carols (with all the tunefulness of a drunk), and refusing to leave until they were paid off with an appropriate gift, or sometimes just hard cash.

In the traditional wassailers' chant "We Wish You a Merry Christmas," the revellers demand food, in the form of figgy

A Teetotal Wassail

3 liters/6 pints of apple juice
1½ liters/3 pints of peach juice
½ cup of freshly squeezed lemon juice
1 large orange
Cloves
6 cinnamon sticks

Stick the orange with whole cloves (roughly half an inch apart) and bake it in the oven. After half an hour take it out and puncture it in several places with a fork. Place the orange with the other ingredients in a large pot and cover. Bring the mixture to a boil before simmering for half an hour. Pour the hot mixture into your heat-proof punch bowl, adding the orange and cinnamon sticks. (This recipe makes around 30 servings!) As time went on, the alcoholic element of the wassail took over in popularity, with the ceremony eventually being absorbed into the general eat, drink, and be merry ethos of the raucous celebrations.

pudding. The words of the carol include the veiled threat of "We won't go until we get some!" However, in the words of the Gloucestershire Wassail, the threat of physical violence is made perfectly plain:

Come butler, come fill us a bowl of the best
Then we hope that your soul in heaven may rest
But if you do draw us a bowl of the small
Then down shall go butler, bowl and all.

Just as the original pagan wassail ceremony was intended to encourage a bountiful harvest of fruit in the year to come, it was also at Christmastime that wassailers would bless the apple orchards. This practice was most prevalent in the fruit-growing counties of Kent and the West of England, and it took place on Twelfth Night.

In this case it was often cider that filled the wassail cup and, having drunk of it themselves, the orchard owners would then water the roots of the fruit trees with it, in the hope that it would ensure their fertility for the year to come. They would then make as much noise as possible to drive away evil spirits before heading home to get back to the serious business of drinking. In more modern times, in some areas, men would then discharge their shotguns into the branches of the trees, while in Surrey the trunks were whipped!

The practice of wassailing eventually lost favor when the Puritans tried to get rid of Christmas for good. It was the Victorians who really revived the custom, but in the process they converted it into the practice of caroling from door to door that is now so popular. And so, it can be seen that wassail, originally a drink, came to mean the ceremony of which it was an integral part, and from there the song, sung with ale-inspired enthusiasm.

The wooden wassail bowl, or cup, steadily took on greater and greater significance throughout the Medieval period, being decorated with ribbons and greenery. In some parts of England, New Year was celebrated with a wassailing procession. Two young girls bearing the wassail bowl between them would lead the procession from house to house, inviting those they visited to partake of the contents of the cup before refilling it with their own supply of alcohol.

> Our wassail cup is made of the rosemary tree,
> And so is your beer of the best barley.
> Call up the butler of this house
> Put on his golden ring;
> Let him bring us up a glass of beer,
> And better we shall sing.

WHO WAS GOOD KING WENCESLAS?

A popular carol sung each Christmas is "Good King Wenceslas." Traditionally reserved for the Feast of Saint Stephen's Day (December 26), it tells the story of the aforementioned good king looking out of his castle to see a poor man foraging for firewood in the forest. In an act of Christian charity, Wenceslas decides to spread the Christmas cheer and sets off with his page, into the cold and the dark, to make sure that the wretch enjoys himself to the full. But who was the real-life inspiration for the saintly monarch, and was good King Wenceslas as good as the carol would have us believe?

Well, first of all you can discard the narrative from the carol as fact, as it was invented by that infamous Victorian caroler, J. M. Neale, in 1853. Neale was the translator of both the Advent hymn "O come, O come, Emmanuel" and the popular carol "Good Christian Men Rejoice." When it came to "Good King Wenceslas," he took what was originally the tune of a springtime carol, "*Tempus adest floridum*," to provide his saccharin-sweet festive number with a melody.

You'll be relieved to hear that Wenceslas did at least exist, although he wasn't a king. He was actually a duke, but you could call him a prince if you were feeling generous. Born circa AD 907, in Stochov near Prague, in what is now the Czech Republic, he was ruler of the principality of Bohemia. He was raised as a Christian by his grandmother Saint Ludmilla. His mother, Drahomíra, was a pagan, and ruthlessly ambitious. She had Ludmilla murdered and then ruled as regent herself until Wenceslas came of age. However, intrigue plagued her court and a desire on the behalf of the populace of Bohemia to see an end to the conflicts between the Christian and non-Christian factions within the region led to Wenceslas taking the reins of government himself.

As a mark of his pious Christian upbringing, it is said that Wenceslas took a vow of virginity and that German missionary priests, seeking to make Bohemia Christian, enjoyed his whole-hearted support. By AD 929, Christianity was spreading throughout Bohemia, but Wenceslas' own converting zeal upset his non-Christian rivals. That same year, faced with the threat of invasions from Germany, Wenceslas submitted to the German king, Henry I. This upset the nobles still further, who then plotted to get rid of him. These same nobles colluded with Wenceslas' own brother, Boleslav, who waylaid him on the way to mass. Boleslav cut him down at the door to the church, hacking him to pieces. Wenceslas was only twenty-two years old.

Almost as soon as he was buried, there came reports of miracles taking place at Wenceslas' tomb. In AD 932, fear full of reprisals from beyond the grave, the superstitious Boleslav had his dead brother's remains disinterred and moved to the church of Saint Vitus, in Prague itself. The church was a popular pilgrimage site during Medieval times and eventually became a cathedral. Wenceslas himself was canonized and made patron saint of Bohemia.

5c

United States Postage

WHY DO PEOPLE KISS
UNDER THE MISTLETOE?

Like so many others, stealing a kiss under the mistletoe is one of those traditions that are a hangover of our pre-Christian past. Both the Ancient Greeks and the druidic priests of the Celtic peoples revered the mistletoe, believing it to have supernatural healing properties. To the Romans the mistletoe was a symbol of peace and used as part of the Saturnalia celebrations.

Like other plants that remained green all year long, it was taken as a symbol of prosperity and fruitfulness. Thoughts of fertility returning to the land, especially during the seemingly lifeless days of midwinter, were foremost in the minds of the early peoples who relied on the bounteous gifts of the earth for their immediate survival.

In Norse mythology, the plant was sacred to Frigga (also known as Freya) who was the goddess of love. It was an arrow crafted from mistletoe wood that shot and killed Frigga's beloved son, Balder, the god of light, and this legend is just one possible source of the practice of kissing under the mistletoe. Following Balder's death, Frigga mourned his passing by sobbing her heart out. The tears that fell from her eyes transformed into the pearly white berries of the mistletoe. She then proceded to kiss everyone who passed under the oak tree where the plant grew, instructing them that whenever they met beneath the mistletoe they should kiss one another in peace, rather than do each other harm.

As far as the Celtic druids were concerned, mistletoe retained its magical properties only if it was cut from a sacred oak where it grew using a golden sickle. It was then allowed to fall from the tree but was caught in a white cloth before it touched the ground. The fact that the plant grew completely off the ground was the reason for the druids' great respect for it.

They imagined that because it apparently grew out of nothing it must have magical properties.

The name we know it by comes from two Anglo-Saxon words and reveals precisely how the mistletoe can grow where it does. *Mistel* is the Anglo-Saxon for "dung" and *tan* means "a small branch." Birds (usually the mistle thrush) feast on the mistletoe's berries, then, having had their fill, they do what everyone does after a big meal—they void their bowels. The seeds excreted in this way germinate in the bark of the tree and a new mistletoe plant grows.

To complete the druids' ritual, two white bulls were sacrificed as a prayer was said. Quite a performance, but as far as the druids were concerned it was worth it. The mistletoe was called the "all-healer." Among its supposed powers, it was believed to be a remedy against poison and to make barren animals fertile again.

These beliefs persisted into Medieval times, when it was fed to cattle to make sure they calved in the spring, and any woman hoping to fall pregnant would carry a sprig of it about her person. It was also considered an effective treatment for toothache, nervous disorders, epilepsy, heart disease, and snakebites. It was also somehow supposed to bring quarrels to an end and was a sure means of protection against witches and lightning strikes! (One strongly held belief had it that mistletoe was formed when lightning struck a tree.)

Today, mistletoe is becoming rarer in this country for, as well as oak, it particularly likes to grow on apple trees, and apple orchards have been shrinking in size and number throughout England over the last half century at an alarming rate. Much of the mistletoe you see on sale at Christmas will have been imported from Normandy.

The more modern practice of kissing under the mistletoe can be traced back to eighteenth-century England. Young women who stood underneath the mistletoe could not refuse a kiss, and if any unfortunate girl remained unkissed under the berries it was said that she would not marry during the coming year. In one version of the custom, every time a young man stole a kiss from a girl he plucked a berry from the mistletoe bough. When all the berries had been plucked, the privilege ceased, as is recalled by this ditty:

Pick a berry off the mistletoe
For ev'ry kiss that's given.
When the berries have all gone,
There's an end to the kissing.

At one stage, during the Medieval period, a new legend sprang up briefly that the cross on which Christ had been crucified was made from mistletoe—rather than holly, as a previous legend had stated—because at that time people believed that the mistletoe had once been a tree itself. The story went that the mistletoe was so ashamed of the use to which it had been put that it shrank to become the parasitic plant we know today and, at the same time, was denied any contact with the ground. In Brittany, France, the plant is still known as *Herbe de la Croix* ("herb of the cross") because of this association.

It is likely that this legend drew from the Norse myth of the death of Balder, in which the mistletoe had then also been the innocent means of the Norse god's death. This attempt to Christianize the

pagan mistletoe, however, was not successful and the plant was forbidden to be brought into any church building. The exception to this rule was York Minster, where a large bunch of mistletoe was laid on the altar every Christmas.

It was once the case that Christmas decorations, including boughs of mistletoe, were treated with great respect. It was considered extreme bad luck to throw them away—you didn't even dare let any piece fall onto the floor—and instead they were burnt or fed to cows. However, the mistletoe bough was carefully put away until it was time for a new one to replace it in twelve

Did you know . . . ?

Duke Guillaume of Normandy was crowned King William I of England in Westminster Abbey on Christmas Day 1066.

Today, this once favored feast is barely celebrated at all, instead becoming a rather gloomy affair, an anticlimax of a day when the Christmas tree, cards, and other decorations are taken down. However, there are some Twelfth Night traditions which have lasted the test of time and are still practiced today.

One of these is the service held at St James' Palace, London, attended by the royal family. At this service, members of the royal household present the Chapel Royal with the three gifts brought to the Christ child by the Magi. Another tradition, upheld by the cast of the play then being performed at the Theatre Royal Drury Lane at that time, is the eating of the Baddeley Cake.

This is as a result of a stipulation made in the last will and testament of one Robert Baddeley, an actor from the eighteenth century, after whom the cake is named.

months' time. In this part of the country mistletoe was once associated with New Year rather than Christmas and was not put up until New Year's Eve:

Forth to the wood did merry-men go,
To gather in the mistletoe.
(From 'Old Christmas' by Walter Scott)

In the West of England, Twelfth Night is the time when wassailing ceremonies are carried out.

At one time in England, Twelfth Night was known as being an appropriate occasion on which to carry out various good luck rituals, as well as for its religious processions which almost went hand-in-hand with the spirited, and genial, revels. Some of these rituals were linked to the countryside and farming, seeing as how, in England's past, people's lives were so strongly connected to the land and the ever-changing seasons.

One of them had farmers lighting bonfires to drive evil spirits away from their farms and fields, the drunken agriculturalists cheering as they circled the fires to hasten the hobgoblins on their way.

There was also the time-honored guessing game, whereby the (now probably inebriated) farmer had to guess what was being roasted in the kitchen before being permitted to reenter his own home. This was not as easy as it might sound, because his good wife might have something as ridiculously inedible as a shoe turning on the spit.

And then there were the Morris men dancing in the streets, as well as fools, hobbyhorses and all. Practical jokes were the name of the game on Twelfth Night, as was the playing of games—particularly games of chance—with everyone determined to make the most of the last day of the holiday season.

Having taken down the Christmas cards and decorations for another year, Twelfth Night presented one last opportunity for a knees-up, the highlight being the cutting of the twelfth-cake. The renowned diarist Samuel Pepys wrote about the celebrations in his household. In an entry from 1668 he writes of offering his guests "an excellent cake which cost me near twenty shillings, of our Jane's making, which was cut into twenty pieces, there being by that time so many of our company."

Once everyone had enjoyed the cake made by Pepys' servant, they partied until 2 AM, dancing and singing. The diarist also mentions that his neighbors joined them in this carousing, but then, from the sounds of it, they probably had little choice. It was either go round to the Pepyses' and join in the fun or spend a sleepless night in bed being kept awake by the party going on next door!

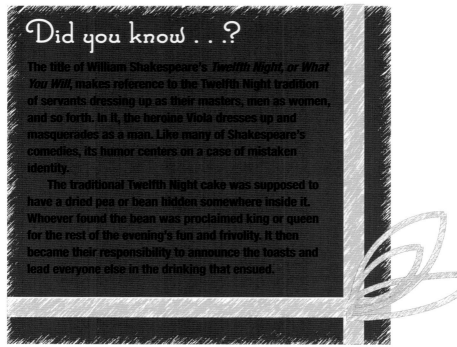

Did you know . . .?

The title of William Shakespeare's *Twelfth Night, or What You Will*, makes reference to the Twelfth Night tradition of servants dressing up as their masters, men as women, and so forth. In it, the heroine Viola dresses up and masquerades as a man. Like many of Shakespeare's comedies, its humor centers on a case of mistaken identity.

The traditional Twelfth Night cake was supposed to have a dried pea or bean hidden somewhere inside it. Whoever found the bean was proclaimed king or queen for the rest of the evening's fun and frivolity. It then became their responsibility to announce the toasts and lead everyone else in the drinking that ensued.

Twelfth-Cake

175 g/6 oz. flour   *175 g/6 oz. butter*
175 g/6 oz. sugar   *3 eggs*
3 tbs brandy   *340 g/12 oz. currants*
40 g/1½ oz. flaked almonds
25 g/1 oz. orange and lemon peel, finely chopped
1 tbs honey
1 tsp of vinegar

Soften the butter and add to the sugar and cream in a mixing bowl. Cream the mixture until light and fluffy. Add the eggs, one at a time, beating well; also add a tablespoon of flour to stop them from curdling. Pour in the brandy, followed by the flour and then the spices. Fold them all in, keeping the mixture light and airy. Lastly stir in the currants, almonds, peel, and honey. The mixture needs to be poured into a prepared cake tin, which is when you can also add a pea or bean, if you wish (but **do not** use a kidney bean, as if it is undercooked it can prove toxic!). Bake for two hours until the cake has browned on top.

However, some kings and queens also earned themselves the responsibility of covering the bill the next day. In time, the bean became a silver sixpence which was cooked inside the Christmas pudding rather than the cake.

The baking of the twelfth-cake brought out the competitive natures of London shopkeepers during the nineteenth century, with rival firms trying to outdo each other in terms of quantity as much as quality. In 1811, one Adams of Cheapside made the bold claim that his cake "considerably surpasses in size any  that has hitherto been made in London, or in fact the world." He went on to say that the monster confection weighed close to half a ton and had been made using "two and a half hundredweight of currants and upwards of a thousand eggs."

However, the twelfth-cake had had its day and the tradition was beginning to die out around the country. Instead it was replaced by the Christmas cake, which actually made use of many of the same ingredients. One of the last twelfth-cakes was made for Queen Victoria by one Mr. Mawditt, the First Yeoman of the Confectionery, in 1849. It was decorated with a scene of an eighteenth-century picnic. However, it was Queen Victoria who helped set the trend for large, rich fruitcakes. The firm of Gunter and Wand made her such a cake for her wedding in February 1840, and so it became popular to have rich fruitcakes made for weddings in general. However, it is unlikely that those that came after Victoria's were ten feet in diameter! Another hundred smaller cakes were also made for Victoria and Albert's wedding, which were given to the royal couple's friends.

Mrs. Beeton (1836–1865) is arguably one of the most famous cookery writers in history, and among the many recipes that she has handed down to us is one for that most seasonal of treats. So rather than using the scribbled recipe handed down from your grandmother this year, why not try Mrs. Beeton's take on the cake for a change?

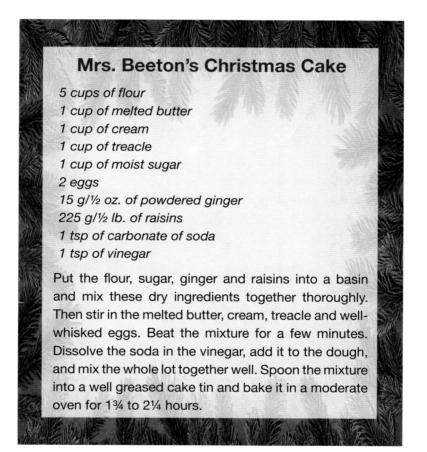

Mrs. Beeton's Christmas Cake

5 cups of flour
1 cup of melted butter
1 cup of cream
1 cup of treacle
1 cup of moist sugar
2 eggs
15 g/½ oz. of powdered ginger
225 g/½ lb. of raisins
1 tsp of carbonate of soda
1 tsp of vinegar

Put the flour, sugar, ginger and raisins into a basin and mix these dry ingredients together thoroughly. Then stir in the melted butter, cream, treacle and well-whisked eggs. Beat the mixture for a few minutes. Dissolve the soda in the vinegar, add it to the dough, and mix the whole lot together well. Spoon the mixture into a well greased cake tin and bake it in a moderate oven for 1¾ to 2¼ hours.

WHY IS CHRISTMAS
SO OFTEN SHORTENED
TO XMAS?

Xmas (sometimes X-mas) is a common abbreviated form of Christmas, usually pronounced "eks-mas." Because it removes the word Christ from Christmas, some people believe it to be irreverent, but how did such a practice come about?

In fact, it dates back further than you might suspect, and has nothing to do with devaluing the Christian festival at all. In reality, both "Christ" and "Christmas" have been abbreviated for at least 1,000 years. The word "Christ" appears in Medieval documents as both "XP" and "Xt" and can even be found in this form in the Anglo-Saxon Chronicle from 1021. But why were those particular letters used?

Some believe the "X" is used as a symbol of the cross on which Christ died, but it is not the case. For early Christians, simply *being* a Christian was a dangerous business. The persecution of those who professed to the worship of Christ by the Romans was at its height, and the stories of Christians being thrown to the lions in Rome's Coliseum have become the stuff of legend. To

live and worship in such times required no small amount of subterfuge on the part of early Christians. To communicate with other like-minded individuals they employed all sorts of signs and symbols which, to the uninitiated, would have meant nothing. These signs and symbols included the fish (employed because the letters of the Greek word for fish, *ichthys*, taken in order, were the initial letters of the phrase Ἰησοῦς Χριστός, Θεοῦ Υἱός, Σωτηρ, meaning "Jesus Christ, God's Son, Savior") and the *labrum*, made up of the letters "X" and "P."

"X" and "P" are the capital forms of the first two letters of the Greek spelling of Christ (or Χριστός) and, as a result, should be pronounced "chi" and "rho." These two letters are often seen merged together, with one letter over the top of the other, in the form of the *labrum*, in churches around the world, particularly

those of the Catholic, Protestant, and Orthodox denominations. By the fifteenth century, "Xmas" was widely used as an abbreviation of "Christmas," in part due to the invention of the printing press by Johannes Gutenberg, in around 1436. This new-fangled machine used moveable type, giving the printer much greater flexibility and a quicker work rate. That said, to

set the type was still a tedious, time-consuming, and expensive job, as it was completed by hand. As a result, abbreviations were common in all manner of publications, including religious ones. In fact, the Church itself used the capital letter "X" in place of the word Christ, to cut the printing costs of books and pamphlets. Newspapers and other publications followed suit, substituting not only "X" for "Christ" and "Xmas" for "Christmas," but also "Xian" for "Christian" and "Inanity" for—you guessed it—"Christianity."

So you can see, the use of "Xmas" in place of "Christmas" is not solely a modern practice and it is certainly not part of a conspiracy to cross Christ out of the festive season, or for secular, commercially driven celebrations to usurp the Christian holiday. It is simply another of those ancient Christmas traditions that has been forgotten with the passage of time.

And, on that note, I would like to wish you a very merry Xmas!

So we keep the olden greeting
With its meaning deep and true,
And wish a merrie Christmas
And a happy New Year to you.

(Old English saying)